Shortcut to IELTS

Reading and Writing

Philip Biggerton

John Ross

Shortcut to IELTS

Reading and Writing

Copyright © 2014 by Phil Biggerton and John Ross

ISBN: 978-0-9575541-1-5

For further information e-mail the authors at:

Godivabooks@gmail.com

The Authors

Phil Biggerton

Phil Biggerton has been teaching English in Asia since 1992. He became an IELTS examiner for the British Council in Taiwan and has spent over twelve years developing his skills as an IELTS teacher. He established Godiva Books Publishing Company in 2010 and since then has published both fiction and non-fiction books for other authors as well as his own textbooks.

John Ross

John Ross is from Auckland, New Zealand. He's been teaching English and writing for twenty years. John has lived in Mongolia, England, and, for the past ten years, Taiwan. Among his many textbooks is the official test preparation series "Step To" for Anglia Examinations. In his free time, John enjoys reading history and travel books, and working on his small farm.

Acknowledgements

We would like to thank the following teachers and schools for their help in developing and testing the material in this book:

Faren Aicel, Mary Aninon, Justin Blake, Faida Bojos, Steven Crook, Rukawa Echizen, Dan Estillore, Hannah Estillore, Diomel Estrera, Charismae Ferrer, Yhang Garcia, Rowan Hunter, Neva Kohl, Joe Lopez, Vienna Mac, Shelsa Maglasang, Clifford Malinao, Troy Parfitt, Christina Peek, Nino Peak, Hezel Rosapa, Alan Rudderham, Joan Tumulak, Jecil Tunacao, Donna Tung, Wilma D Wil-an, Melani Ygsi, David's English Center, Excel Language Learning Center, Genius English Academy, Joinus English Language Academe, and RTC English.

Contents

Contents

How to use Shortcut to IELTS

Although the book covers two skills – Reading and Writing – it is organised into three basic parts; Reading, Task One Writing and Task Two Writing. The two IELTS writing tasks have been separated, Task One in the first half and Task Two in the second half of the book. Many IELTS test takers find the first writing task, which typically involves describing a chart, the most difficult part of the test. Because of this, we have focused on it in great detail, covering all the kinds of possible questions, and going through the writing process step-by-step. The Task Two Writing also follows a step-by-step approach, so it is important that you work through these skills in order.

There is so much material in **Shortcut to IELTS** that, if it is used as a classroom textbook, some of it is best assigned as homework.

General Advice

Practice Makes Perfect. Practice not only improves your English, but it also allows you to complete questions more quickly. IELTS has a lot of time pressure (many students struggle to complete the writing and reading sections in the time allowed), so being able to do these sections quickly is important. Some of the practice should be "timed practice," i.e. done in the same amount of time as the test allows.

Take Responsibility for your Own Learning. Don't be a passive learner. Don't rely completely on teachers and textbooks to help you. The key to success is the effort that you put in. Try to be an active learner. Speak up in class, and practise at home. Pay attention to the kind of mistakes you make. Think about your weaknesses and what you need to do to improve in those areas.

Don't be Discouraged. The first time you see IELTS test material, you may feel discouraged. The test looks very hard. Don't worry; even your English teacher felt confused the first time he or she saw it. It will become easier as you become more familiar with IELTS. And remember; you only need to get a little more than half of the questions right to get a good score.

Interpreting a Chart

Line charts, bar charts and tables often show changes over a period of time, and how quickly or how slowly these changes happen. They can also tell you how big or how small these changes are.

A lot of the information you are likely to see in the IELTS Task 1 writing test can be expressed using two lines, the x-axis (horizontal) and the y-axis (vertical). This forms a chart where the rest of the information can be added.

Task 1

x-axis

This will usually show the passing of time in:

- Hours
- Days
- Weeks
- Months
- Years or even decades

y-axis

This will show what changes over a period of time:

- The number of cars exported to the US
- The cost of public transportation
- The amount of electricity used per household, etc.

The charts below show the number of staff in the engineering department at two universities.

Bar Chart

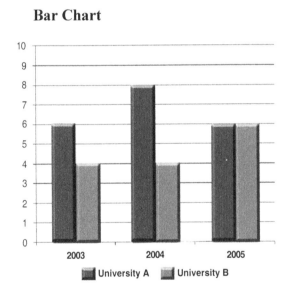

Line Chart

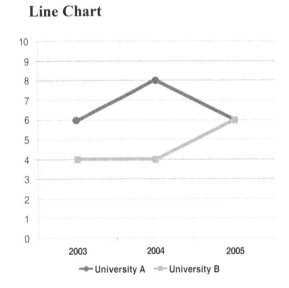

Exercise

Note that the bar chart and line chart show exactly the same information. Use the information in the bar chart and line chart above to complete the table below.

Table

	2003	2004	2005
University A			
University B			

Writing the Introduction

When writing the introduction, it is useful to remember that you are answering the question, "What is it?" In other words, "What type of information does the chart show?" The more clearly you answer this question, the better your introduction is likely to be. Many students, however, when they first start studying how to write this type of essay, only make slight changes to the Task 1 introduction given to them. This would not please the examiner.

Task 1
The diagram below shows information on the average individual drinking habits in a coffee shop in Manchester.

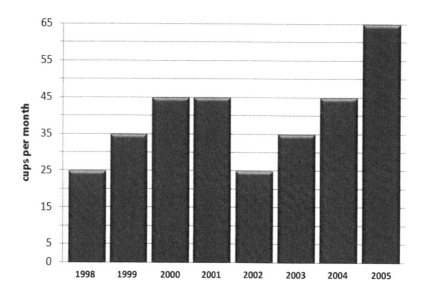

Make sure you look for:

- ♦ the type of chart - bar chart, line chart, table, and so on
- ♦ a time period. Remember that not all charts have time periods
- ♦ the type and number of categories
- ♦ the units

Exercise
Pick the best introduction for this diagram from the list below. What do you like or dislike about each sentence? What would you change and why?

1. The bar chart provides data on the number of coffee consumed per person per month in a typical Manchester coffee shop over a 7-year period from 1998 to 2005.

2. The chart presents information on the amount of coffee in a typical Manchester coffee shop.

3. The bar chart provides information on the average amount of coffee consumed per person in a typical month in a Manchester coffee shop over an 8-year period from 1998 to 2005.

4. The bar chart below shows that monthly consumption of coffee in a Manchester coffee shop over a 8-year period from 1998 to 2005.

Writing the Introduction

The best introduction for the Task 1 diagram on page 8 is sentence number three:

> *The bar chart provides information on the average amount of coffee consumed per person in a typical month in*
>
> *a Manchester coffee shop over an 8-year period from 1998 to 2005.*

It contains all of the basic information that the examiner looks for and also shows an ability to use the phrase – *the amount of* – correctly.

Many students get confused with – **the amount of/the number of/levels of** – and make mistakes. Practise this skill by completing the exercise below.

Exercise
It is important to be able to use these phrases properly and in the correct order. Look at the table below and see if you can match the different categories with the right grammatical expression. Note that many words can be used more than once.

the number of …..	the amount of …..	levels of …..

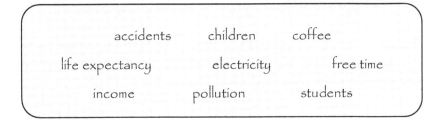

accidents   children   coffee

life expectancy   electricity   free time

income   pollution   students

Exercise
Now, write two Task 1 introductions by using each sentence below and the extra information provide in brackets.

1. The chart below shows information about different cities and their population.

(1997-2007/New York, Tokyo, London, Rome/table)

2. The chart below shows Internet usage in various states in America.

(1985-2003/California, Oregon, Florida, Colorado, Ohio, Alaska/bar chart)

Writing the General Statement

After writing the introduction, you now need to write the general statement. This provides the main idea or trend of the diagram.

Remember: no figures are used when writing this sentence.

Exercise
Look closely at the table you completed on page 7 again and decide what would make a good general statement.

Exercise
Try to decide which universities have experienced an increase in the number of staff in the table below.

Task 1
The chart below shows the number of staff in the engineering department at three universities.

	2003	2004	2005	2006	2007
University A	6	8	6	9	8
University B	8	10	8	10	9
University C	5	7	6	8	3

As you look more closely at what happened over the 5 years, from 2003 to 2007, you can see that the number of staff in each university has fluctuated. You can not, however, write things like;

The number of staff went up and down ... / The number of staff fluctuated ...

These statements, although true, are not good general statements. To find a trend for each university, simply look at the number of staff employed in 2003 and then the number of staff in 2007. DO NOT look at any of the other years. Did employment figures increase or decrease for each university?

You should have found that, University A increased, University B increased, and University C decreased. This information can now be turned into a general statement;

In general, staff in the engineering departments of Universities A and B rose but figures fell for University C over this period of time.

If you wanted to write about a main idea what could this be?

Exercise
Look at the table again and see if one university always, or nearly always, had more staff than the others.

University B had more staff in every year and so this could be used to write a general statement with a main idea:

An overview of this chart shows that University B always had more staff than the other two universities over this period of time.

Main Body

To be able to write a good main body, it is important to become familiar with the vocabulary that is commonly used to describe diagrams. Unlike Writing Task 2, which we will begin to look at in Unit 9, Task 1 needs very little in the way of vocabulary. The main skills that you need to develop are the ability to describe and analyse a diagram.

When we write about the main body for a chart we often have to write about things going up and things going down. As a piece of writing, it becomes very boring if we keep reading, *it went up*, *it went down*, *it went up again* and so on. We need to find other words that can be used instead of the very informal (non-academic) UP and DOWN.

Exercise
Complete the diagram by reading the main body text then discuss your answers with a classmate.

Task 1
The diagram below shows changes in pollen in New York in 2012. Read the main body below the diagram and draw in the information for San Francisco.

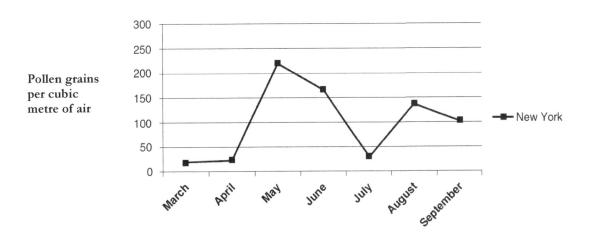

More specifically, pollen levels in New York rose dramatically from slightly below 25 pollen grains per cubic metre of air in March and April to just under 225 in May. During the same period of time levels in San Francisco increased from exactly 150 to a little under 175 in April but then fell rapidly to just under 100 the following month. This trend then continued and figures dropped to a little below 75 in June. Similarly, the amount of pollen in New York also declined with a drop, from May to June, of almost exactly 50 grains per cubic metre of air. This was followed by a substantial decrease to just over 25 in July. However, levels in San Francisco climbed to exactly 100 in July and a little over 200 in August. This trend was mirrored in New York with a rise of a little over 100 grains. Both New York and San Francisco experienced a drop in pollen in the final month to a little over 100 and a little over 175 respectively.

Exercise
Now try to write the introduction and general statement.

Main Body – Adjectives and Adverbs

Many students often get confused about how to use adjectives and adverbs. Using these correctly will impress the examiner and will help to increase your grade.

Exercise
Look at the exercise below and decide which sentences are correct.

1.
A There was a slightly decrease
B Sales decreased slightly
C Sales went down

2.
A Pollution levels fell rapid
B Rapidly pollution levels dropped
C Levels of pollution dropped rapidly

3.
A Sales no change in 2000
B Sales remained stable at 2000
C Sales stable at 2000

4.
A Sales dropped dramatic to 1000
B Sales were dropped to 1000
C Sales fell dramatically from 3000 to 1000

Exercise
Now complete the six sentences below by using some of the words in brackets.

1. _____ sales _____ in New York from US$165,000 in 2003 to US$132,000 in 2010, figures _____ higher than all of the other five cities.
(felled / fell / falling /interestingly / stay / remained / despite)

2. The percentage of women majoring in science subjects _____ _____ from 7% to 8% over this period of time.
(increase / increased / slight / slightly / decreased / significantly)

3. Levels of pollution _____ _____ from 1200 metric tons in 2007 to 3000 metric tons in 2010; a climb of 1800 metric tons.
(increase / rose / dramatic / dramatically / climb / slight)

4. The number of accidents in school playgrounds _____ by 15% over the five years; _____ _____ from 27% to 12%.
(rose / fell / decrease / decreasing / increase / substantial / substantially)

5. Travelling by bus also _____ with the total mileage _____ from 540,000 miles in 2001 to 235,000 miles 7 years later.
(drop / dropped / fall / falling / steady / went down)

6. Generally speaking, salaries were _____ _____ in Europe than in Asia.
(significant / significantly / high / higher)

Introduction to Reading

The reading part of the test is made up of three reading passages with a total of forty questions to answer in one hour. Unlike the listening test, where you have an extra ten minutes to transfer your answers from the question sheet to the answer sheet, answers for the reading test must be transferred to the answer sheet by the end of the sixty minutes. No extra time is allowed.

There are three things that can make reading more difficult:

- ♦ the type of topic
- ♦ the type of question
- ♦ the instructions

The Topics

The topics change from passage to passage and from test to test. You might find, for instance, that reading passage one is about spiders, passage two about living underground, and passage three about making light bulbs. How wide your vocabulary range is will help determine how difficult you think each passage is. Being more prepared means having a wider vocabulary range.

Take every opportunity to read. Read labels on food you might buy from the supermarket, read the headlines of a newspaper as you walk past a newsstand, leave the radio on when you are cleaning your teeth, watch a movie in your free time, or go to a bookstore and buy a book to read; biographies are good as they can be quite motivational as well as offer a wide range of vocabulary.

The Questions

The type of question – and there are over 12 different question types – will also influence your feeling about the test and can have a big effect on your final grade. Although it is possible to generalize and say that, for example, YES, NO, NOT GIVEN questions are harder than sentence completion type questions, everyone is different and what is easy for one might be very difficult for another.

With over 12 questions types that could be in the test, it is anyone's guess which question types you will find in your test. This means you must study all of them and try to become good at every type of question. If, for instance, you want to get a grade 6.0 in reading – approximately 24 out of 40 – you should try to get at least 60% correct for all question types.

The Instructions

The instructions are the final point to consider here. The problem is not that they are difficult to understand but that students forget to read them. It is very common for students to begin to think that instructions never change and so they stop reading them. This is a big mistake – they do change and they often change when you least expect them to. One set of questions might, for instance, say:

*Choose **ONE WORD ONLY** from the passage for each answer.*

but another might say:

*Write **NO MORE THAN THREE WORDS AND/OR A NUMBER** for each answer.*

Remember: the reading passages are **NOT** in order of difficulty.

Reading – **Question Types** – Multiple Choice

One common question type is multiple choice. This is where you are given one question and have to choose the correct answer from three or four possible answers. Multiple choice does not mean that you can choose more than one answer. This will only happen if the instructions clearly say, for instance; *Choose **TWO** letters, A–E.*

Remember: as stated before – read the instructions – **ALWAYS**.

Travel is the best form of education

One learns a lot while serving in the United States Army. Foreign places, stressful conditions, and absence from home can foster an out-of-the-classroom education that crosses the boundary of the odd and unusual. Today, tales of strange sea creatures and haunted islands seem like a bad Sci-Fi marathon. But these were realities for one U.S. Army soldier stationed overseas at the turn of the 20th century.

The arts of journal keeping, letter writing and daily diary entries are becoming extinct as methods of memory management in today's technology driven world. What once was detailed on paper with memory fresh at hand is now posted on YouTube. Today, blogs replace the diary entries. Hand-written letters to loved ones are far slower than a quick Facebook 'poke' or a cell phone text message.

Historians enjoy a deep appreciation for the written word. They savor the ability to see the world through the eyes of someone who never had satellite TV, the Internet or a cell phone. Where explanation was not readily at hand in the strange lands of the Philippine Islands, the environment was ripe for adventure and the unknown. Placing one's self into such situations fosters an education that cannot be duplicated in any classroom, book or blockbuster movie. A survivor of deadly and savage situations, Colonel Horace P. Hobbs recorded these well-documented experiences that lend a degree of depth to the retelling and re-imagining of Army history.

The odd education of Colonel Horace P. Hobbs is revealed in his voluminous personal papers held at the U.S. Army Military History Institute. A letter of August 16, 1918, soothes his wife while he is stationed in France during World War I. "You see it is the women who suffer most during war. Now I know you and mother are worrying about me and I am living in the most luxurious comfort and perfect safety just now." He goes to great length to explain his lush surroundings and the comfort he is experiencing, from bathing in a nearby brook, to the size of his room and the servants who provide for him, as he attempts to console a worry-sick wife. It would seem, however, that Mrs. Hobbs had been through worse as a military spouse.

Her husband was stationed in the Philippines during the insurrection from 1899 to 1901. Colonel Hobbs wrote a book from his collected journals and memoirs entitled, *"Kris and Krag: Adventures among the Moros of the Southern Philippine Islands"*. Among his many tales, the Colonel tells about a strange native custom on one of the small islands of taking their boats across a narrow strait to another island and returning before dark. They explained to him that the island was the home of the 'wok-wok', a powerful ghost who must be appeased with gifts of rice so they will not harm the people. Upon further inspection the Army discovered the 'wok-wok' to be large apes.

Another bizarre chapter in the Colonel's education came when he was asked by some villagers to kill a sea creature which wreaked havoc among the people whenever they slaughtered an animal for food. The blood would run into the water, and out would come the creature. The Colonel waited for the apparition to appear after a slaughter, and he was not disappointed. Upon further inspection he described the animal as being some kind of mix between an alligator and a crocodile, but one he had never seen before.

Experience in foreign places, blended with curiosity and a desire to learn, enabled Colonel Hobbs to obtain a far greater grasp of the world. These traits provided him with an education that the average person today cannot obtain from watching television or searching the web.

Questions 1–5

*Choose the correct letter, **A**, **B**, **C** or **D***

1. What offers a non-traditional form of education?

   A being away from home

   B being in foreign countries

   C situations that cause stress

   D all of the above

2. Historians enjoy the chance to see

   A satellite TV.

   B the world through others' eyes.

   C the world.

   D well-documented experiences.

3. In France the Colonel

   A looked after his sick wife.

   B lived with his wife.

   C wrote letters to the U.S. Army Military History Institute.

   D comforted his wife with his letters.

4. A sea creature would appear

   A whenever the Colonel was in the village.

   B and make the Colonel disappointed.

   C when blood from a dead animal ran into the water.

   D and slaughter an animal.

5. What traits helped give the Colonel a good education?

   A a desire to travel to foreign places

   B a good grasp of the world and curiosity

   C watching TV and using the Internet

   D a desire to learn and curiosity

Reading – Multiple Choice

Cheng Man-ch'ing – Tai Chi Master

As a young man Cheng Man-ch'ing suffered from tuberculosis and while receiving treatment for his condition he developed an interest in traditional Chinese medicine. Cheng started to study traditional Chinese medicine with the famous Tai Chi master Yang Ch'eng-fu in 1932. Later on, Yang Ch'eng-fu took Cheng Man-ch'ing as his student and taught him the Yang Tai Chi system. This has now become known as the Yang Long Form and consists of 108 movements.

Cheng went on to become a professor and then taught Tai Chi at a military academy. While at the academy he found he could not teach the complete Yang Long Form to the soldiers in the time allocated. He, therefore, looked for a way to shorten the form that would allow the soldiers to learn it in less time. By 1947 Professor Cheng had simplified the original form by removing many of the repetitive movements. This process reduced the total number of individual non-repetitive movements to 37 and the form still retained the skills and essence of the longer form. In 1949 the Communists took control of China and Professor Cheng Man-ch'ing fled with his family to Taiwan. While there he established himself as a teacher and taught the Short Yang Tai Chi or Cheng Man-ch'ing 37 Posture Form, as well as painting, poetry and calligraphy.

In 1964 he travelled to New York and continued to teach Tai Chi. His knowledge and love of Tai Chi was and still is an example and has inspired many students to spread his name and innovative ideas throughout North America, Europe and the Far East. Today the Cheng Man-ch'ing Form as it is now known is one of the most popular Tai Chi forms outside of China.

Questions 1-3

*Which **THREE** facts are mentioned by the writer of this article?*

- **A** In Taiwan, he only taught Tai Chi.
- **B** He couldn't teach the soldiers in the location he wanted.
- **C** Cheng Man-ch'ing's students helped make him famous. ✓
- **D** Cheng Man-ch'ing eliminated 71 moves from the original form. ✓
- **E** Studying Chinese medicine was Yang Ch'eng-fu's condition for teaching Cheng.
- **F** Limited time resulted in Cheng Man-ch'ing developing a new form of Tai Chi. ✓

Writing Task 1 – **Main Body** – Units

Exercise
Look at the diagram below and write an introduction and general statement. Remember to look for all of the important information. For extra practice try to write both a general statement trend and a general statement main idea.

Task 1
The diagram below shows information on migration into and out of the UK.

	2002	2003	2004	2005	2006	2007	2008	2009
IN	488	518	541	604	581	606	566	562
OUT	345	363	354	340	392	394	375	386
Net Inflow	143	155	186	264	189	212	192	177

(population in thousands)

Did you also remember to look for the units? For instance, how many people moved to the UK in 2006? If you said 581 people then you failed to notice the units – "population in thousands". It is a good idea to look for the units at the same time you look for information for the introduction. You don't need to include the units as part of your introduction but it does ensure you use the correct figures in the main body.

Exercise
To understand units more clearly, complete the table below:

Figures from Chart	Unit	Actual Figure
3.2	'00s	**Example:** 320
95	'00s of radios	
885	in thousands of vehicles	
79.6	millions of viewers a day	
15.3	number of flights in thousands	
56	(%)	
68.7	in hundreds of US$	

Writing Task 1 – **Main Body** – Describing a Diagram

Remember, being able to describe a diagram accurately is an important skill to learn if you want to get a good grade in the IELTS test. It is essential, as you have already seen, that you learn how to use adjectives and adverbs correctly, but it is also important to be able to calculate figures accurately.

For instance, if you look at the diagram below and the figure for 1995, you can see that the figure is exactly 300. Many students still write phrases like – *university admissions in 1995 were roughly 300* – this is wrong. Be accurate and write – *university admissions in 1995 were exactly 300.*

Task 1

UK university admissions from Nepal from 1995 to 2004.

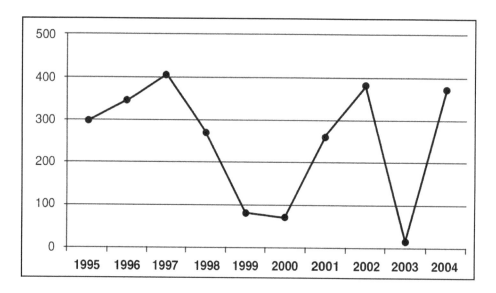

If you now look at 1996, what do you think the figure is? A sentence stating – *university admissions in 1996 were exactly 345* – is too accurate and would be seen by the examiner more as a guess than an accurate analysis of the diagram. You can use phrases like the ones below to write about figures that cannot be expressed with absolute certainty.

- ♦ a little under
- ♦ a little over
- ♦ just under
- ♦ just over
- ♦ slightly less than
- ♦ slightly more than

Exercise

Look at the chart again and write the introduction, general statement and main body by describing what happens each year.

Writing Task 1 – **Main Body** – Accuracy with Numbers

Exercise

The diagram below shows various leisure time activities enjoyed by males and females. Although there is no time period, we do have different age groups. This means that it is still possible to state the trend for each activity. Look at the table and decide how many activities increased and how many decreased. Then write an introduction and general statement.

	21-35	21-35	36-45	36-45	46 +	46+
	male	female	male	female	male	female
Jogging	35%	23%	48%	31%	22%	31%
Baseball	87%	2%	64%	1%	29%	0%
Basketball	97%	22%	68%	15%	43%	3%
Meditation	0%	5%	3%	12%	7%	27%
Fishing	12%	1%	32%	0%	45%	0%
Yoga	3%	7%	7%	33%	7%	42%
Cricket	24%	0%	18%	1%	9%	0%

When writing the general statement you probably realised that there are too many items to list them all. However, you could have written: *Generally speaking, a higher percentage of men participated in these activities apart from mediation and yoga which were favoured by women.*

You can see that in the general statement, the terms *men* and *women* were used to replace *male* and *female* found in the Task 1 introduction. This idea can also be used in the main body to make your writing more interesting.

Exercise

Look at the sample answer below and find other words or expressions that replace the words '*male*' and '*female*'.

> The least preferred activity for males in the 36-45 age group was meditation with 3% participation whereas 12% of all females surveyed did this activity. The biggest overall increase in percentage in any activity for women was for yoga which rose from 7% in the youngest age group to 42% in the oldest age group. The opposite sex, however, experienced the biggest change in fishing from 12% to 45% respectively, a total climb of 33%. No change was seen in jogging at 31% in the two older age groups for women. Similarly, their counterparts saw no variation for yoga which remained at 7% in the same two age groups. It is interesting to note that the biggest difference between the two sexes in any one age group and the same activity was for baseball in the youngest age group; men had 87% whilst the opposite gender had only 2%. **(149 words)**

Exercise

Which sentence or sentences would you remove to reduce the total length? Why?

Writing Task 1 – **Main Body** – Analysing

When we first look at the bar chart shown below it seems as if it is going to be very difficult to analyse. Figures increase in regular steps from 2001 to 2010, and nothing seems to stand out as being very different.

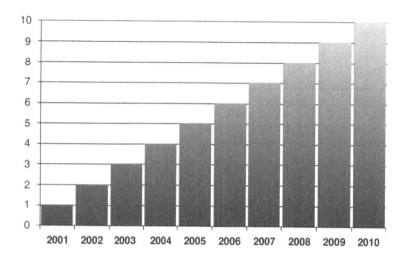

However, to analyse well, it is important to be able to move past the initial impression and start to focus on different parts of the chart. Do not just look at the years in order. Jump from one year to another and see what can be compared and contrasted. You can use a pencil to help you make these connections.

Exercise
Now look at the second bar chart and see how these connections have been made. To make it easier to understand, the actual years have been moved on the x-axis. Now you can see that year 2010 is next to 2001 because they are the largest and smallest respectively. Year 2005 is next because this is exactly half the largest figure.

Exercise
What other connections can you make with this chart? Compare and contrast as many figures as you can.

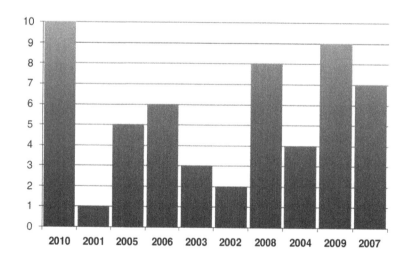

Writing Task 1 – **Main Body** – Analysing

Exercise

Now look at another example and, using ideas from page 20, write the main body. You can also write an introduction and general statement for extra practice. Remember that one figure may not be, for example, "*exactly three times larger*" and so you need to use the phrases shown to you on page 18.

Task 1

The diagram below shows the number of papers accepted for publication from the Engineering Faculty at Warwick University in 2011.

Summarise the information by selecting and reporting the main features, and make comparisons where relevant.

Write at least 150 words.

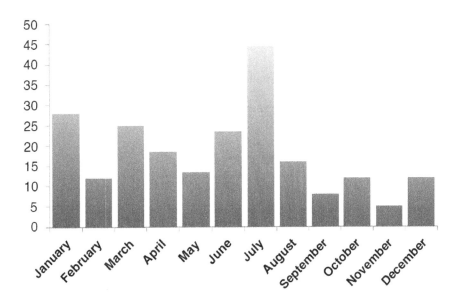

Writing Task 1 – Main Body – Analysing

Here you will begin to look at some of the main features of a diagram that you can look for when writing the main body. What you look for, however, will depend on whether the diagram has a time period or not. A diagram with a time period will focus more on what changes but a diagram with no time period will focus more on comparisons and contrasts.

Exercise

Look at the table below and complete the last two columns indicating what you can look for in each type of diagram. Write YES if you can look for this particular feature and NO if you can not.

	Key Features	Time Period	No Time Period
1.	The extremes (the biggest and the smallest)		
2.	The constant (no change)		
3.	The longest continued rise / fall over a period of time		
4.	The only category to always rise / fall		
5.	A peak		
6.	A trough		
7.	Biggest or smallest increase / Biggest or smallest decrease		
8.	Two categories the same / two points the same in one category		
9.	Comparison between two categories		

Exercise

Now look at the sentences below and match them to the correct key feature above.
For example, **A** matches with key feature number **5**.

A The number of hours people spent watching TV peaked at an average of 6.2 hours per day over the weekend.

B The only category to experience a continued climb in book sales was the UK, increasing from 2.3 million to 4.5 million over this period of time.

C Both Brazil and Argentina had the same literacy levels in 2003 with 98.2%.

D The biggest difference in tourism occurred between Thailand and Cambodia where figures were 4.5 million and 2 million respectively, a difference of 2.5 million.

E The most expensive apartments were in Hong Kong with an average weekly cost of US$1,750.

F City A and City B both had troughs in 2006 where fuel consumption fell to 200 and 125 megawatts respectively.

G Levels of air pollution remained constant at 0.14ppm for 3-consecutive years from 2006-2008.

H The smallest overall decline was in New York where government spending fell by 1.3%.

I The number of employees at Microsoft increased gradually over 8-consecutive years from 542 in 1996 to 2,708 in 2003, the longest rise over this period of time.

Reading – **Matching** – Which Paragraph?

IELTS Tips

Sometimes an example is given. Do not look for this answer again!

Answer all the questions. If you are not sure – guess.

Answers are NOT usually in order.

****

Matching is where you have to match – or pair off – the question information with the correct answer. Instructions might ask you to do such things as deciding which paragraph contains which piece of information, which person said what, completing each sentence by picking the correct ending, and selecting the correct heading for each section or paragraph.

Incredible Journeys

A

The nervous system of the desert ant *Cataglyphis fortis*, with around 100,000 neurons, is about 1 millionth the size of a human brain. Yet, in the featureless deserts of Tunisia, this ant can venture over 100 meters from its nest to find food without becoming lost. Imagine randomly wandering 20 kilometers in the open desert, your tracks obliterated by the wind, then turning around and making a beeline to your starting point - and no GPS allowed! That's the equivalent of what the desert ant accomplishes with its scant neural resources. How does it do it?

B

Jason, a graduate student studying the development of human and animal cognition, discusses a remarkable series of experiments on the desert ant on his blog, *The Thoughtful Animal*. In work spanning more than 30 years, researchers from Rüdiger Wehner's laboratory at the University of Zurich Institute of Zoology carefully tracked the movements of ants in the desert as the insects foraged for food. One of the researchers' key questions was how the ants calculated the direction to their nest.

C

To correct for the possibility that the ants used landmarks as visual cues, despite the relatively featureless desert landscape, the researchers engaged in a bit of trickery. They placed a food source at a distance from a nest, then tracked the nest's ants until the ants found the food. Once the food was found, the ants were relocated from that point so that the way back to their nest was a different direction than it would have been otherwise. The relocated ants walked *away* from the nest, in the same direction they should have walked if they had never been moved. This suggested that the ants are not following features, but orienting themselves relative to an internal navigation system or (as turned out to be the case) the position of the Sun in the sky.

D

No matter how convoluted a route the ants take to find the food, they always return in a straight-line path, heading directly home. The researchers discovered that the ants' navigation system isn't perfect; small errors arise depending on how circuitous their initial route was. But the ants account for these errors as well, by walking in a corrective zigzag pattern as they approach the nest. So how do the ants know how far to travel? It could still be that they are visually tracking the distance they walk. The researchers tested this by painting over the ants' eyes for their return trip, but the ants still walked the correct distance, indicating that the ants are not using sight to measure their journeys.

E

Another possibility is that the ants simply count their steps. In a remarkable experiment published in *Science* in 2006, scientists painstakingly attached 'stilts' made of pig hairs to some of the ants' legs, while other ants had their legs clipped, once they had reached their food target. If the ants counted their steps on the journey out, then the newly short-legged ants should stop short of the nest, while stilted ants should walk past it. Indeed, this is what occurred! Ants count their steps to track their location. (If only you had remembered to do this before you started on your 20-kilometer desert trek!)

F

But other creatures have different navigation puzzles to solve. In a separate post, Jason explains a study showing how maternal gerbils find their nests. When a baby is removed from the nest, the gerbil mother naturally tries to find and retrieve it. Researchers placed one of the babies in a cup at the center of a platform, shrouded in darkness. When the mother found the baby, the platform was rotated. Did she head for the new position of her nest, with its scents and sounds of crying babies? No, she went straight for the spot where the nest had been, ignoring all these other cues. For gerbils, clearly, relying on their internal representation of their environment normally suffices, so the other information goes unheeded.

G

Migratory birds, on the other hand, must navigate over much larger distances, some of them returning to the identical geographic spot year after year. How do they manage that trick? One component, University of Auckland researcher and teacher Fabiana Kubke reports, is the ability to detect the Earth's magnetic field. Though we've known about this avian sixth sense for some time, the location of a bird's magnetic detector is still somewhat of a mystery. Last November, however, a team led by Manuela Zapka published a letter in *Nature* that narrowed the possibilities. Migratory European robins have magnetic material in their beaks, but also molecules called cryptochromes in the back of their eyes that might be used as a sort of compass. The team systematically cut the connections between these two areas and the robins' brains, finding that the ability to orient to compass points was only disturbed when the connection to cryptochromes was disrupted.

H

Much remains to be learned about how birds can successfully migrate over long distances. Unlike ants and gerbils, they can easily correct for large displacements in location and still return to the correct spot.

Questions 1– 6

*This reading passage has eight paragraphs, **A– H**.*

Which paragraph contains the following information?

1. An explanation of how adjustments are made when navigating   **Example D**
2. Recent news about how navigation systems work
3. A comparison of tracking abilities
4. A study showing that scent and sound are not important
5. Explaining the importance of counting
6. A description of how ants navigate

Reading– Question Types – Tables

> ### IELTS Tips
>
> Use examples in the table to help you know how to write answers, e.g. do you need to use capital letters, do you need to add units for numbers and so on.
>
> Answers are usually in order.

A table is a little like a summary. The difference is that in a table the information is usually shown in note form rather than sentences. Answers are often hidden by rephrasing information from the text and using synonyms. Information from several sentences can be combined into one phrase in the table and so you might need to look in more than one sentence in the text for some of the answers. It is important to look for the clues.

As answers are usually in order – this is true for nearly all question types – look at the table and pick a word that you think you will be able to find very easily in the text. As soon as you have found this word then you can start looking for the answers. For instance, if you decide to pick a word connected to question three, answer this first and then work above and below where you found the answer in the text to find the other answers.

The ability to select good keywords from the question is a very important skill to develop. A good keyword is a word that is more likely to be the same in the question and text because it would be impossible (or more difficult) to replace with another word. Good examples of words that make good keywords are:

1. **Capitalized words** – Tokyo, Mitsubishi, Ikehata
2. **Specialized words** (with no synonym) – sake

Numbers can also be used as keywords. However, numbers can be disguised more easily by writing the word rather than using figures or expressing the number in a slightly different way. For instance:

1. 6pm   =   six o'clock
2. 2011   =   the early 21st century
3. 25kg   =   twenty five kilograms

They are, nevertheless, still good to look for and can help save valuable time by answering the questions which are the easiest to answer first. Now look at the following article about salinity and answer the questions that follow.

SALINITY

It has long been recognized that our land uses, including agricultural development, have significantly changed Australia's landscapes and natural systems. However, we have not always appreciated the magnitude of change in the soil, water and nutrient balances, the resultant degradation, the timeframe for these changes to be slowed or reversed, and the costs to the wider Australian community.

Changes to the Australian landscape have resulted in the widespread and rapidly growing problem of dryland salinity. Farmers were among the first to be affected, through salinisation of rivers and agricultural land. Biodiversity, as well as regional and urban infrastructure, such as water supply, roads and buildings are now also at risk. Two broad forms of salinity are recognized in Australia:

Primary or naturally occurring salinity is part of the Australian landscape, and reflects the development of this landscape over time. Examples are the marine plains found around the coastline of Australia, and the salt lakes in central and Western Australia.

Salts are distributed widely across the Australian landscapes. They originate mainly from depositions of oceanic salt from rain and wind. Salt stored in the soil or groundwater is concentrated through evaporation and transpiration by plants. In a healthy catchment, salt is slowly leached downwards and stored below the root zone, or out of the system.

Secondary salinity is the salinisation of land and water resources due to land use impacts by people. It includes salinity that results from water table rises from irrigation systems – irrigation salinity, and from dryland management systems – dryland salinity. Both forms of salinity are due to accelerated rising water tables mobilising salt in the soil. There is no fundamental difference in the hydrologic process.

Where the water balance has been altered due to changing land use (e.g. clearing of native vegetation for broad acre farming or grazing) the excess water entering the water table mobilizes salt which then rises to the land surface. Movement of water drives salinisation processes and may move the stored salt towards the soil surface or into surface water bodies.

Questions 1–13

Complete the table below.

*Choose **NO MORE THAN THREE WORDS** from the reading passage for each answer.*

Two Forms of Salinity	
Primary	**Secondary**
Salinity occurs in 1. ...rivers & agr. land...	This is where salinity is affected by
Oceanic salts are deposited by:	7. ...people...
2. ...rain... and	It includes:
3. ...wind...	8. ...dryland... salinity and
Salt is concentrated via:	9. ...irrigation... salinity caused by water tables
4. ...evaporation... and	10. ...water balance...
5. ...transpiration...	Changes in 11. ...excess water... due to
Salt moves downwards below 6. ...the root zone...	12. ...changing land use...
	causes salt to move to 13. ...the soil surface...

Writing Task 1 – **Main Body** – Analysing

Exercise

Look at the bar chart and start to collect any extra information needed to write the introduction. Also, remember to look for units so that you know what the figures really mean. Now think about a general statement and see if it is possible to write both a general statement trend and a general statement main idea.

You only need to include one type of general statement in your Task 1 essay but being able to write both types helps you to develop your analytical skills. Being able to analyse a diagram properly is essential if you want to get a good grade.

Task 1

The table below shows how far different salesmen travelled in 6 months in 2010.

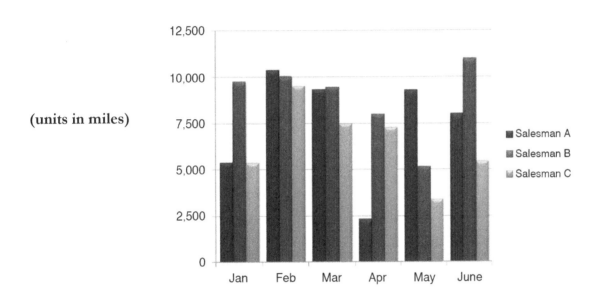

Exercise

Now think about the main body and try (it might not always be possible) to write one sentence for each of the key features listed below. Remember to put figures into each sentence.

Key Features

1. The extremes (the biggest and the smallest)
2. The constant (no change)
3. The longest continued rise / fall over a period of time
4. The only category to always rise / fall
5. A peak
6. A trough
7. Biggest / smallest increase / decrease
8. Two categories the same / two points the same in one category
9. Comparison between two categories

Remember:

Perfect grammar and perfect spelling won't get you a perfect grade if you do not know how to analyse.

Writing Task 1 – **Main Body** – Analysing

Some diagrams use rates as a unit. If you have a diagram like this in your test you must be careful about how you express the figures. For instance, if the diagram shows information on literacy rates in various countries, the units might be expressed as, *literacy rates per 1000 people*. This means that a figure of, for instance, 970 out of 1,000 people are literate. Of course, this could also be expressed as 97% of the people are literate.

Task 1
The diagram below shows information on live births in the UK.

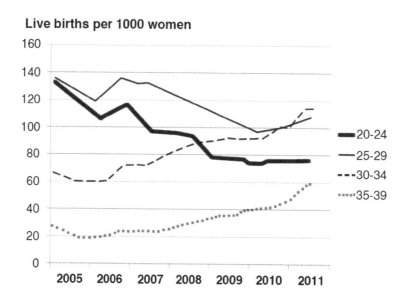

Exercise
Look at the two tables below and match **1–4** with **A–D** to form sentences that describe the line chart. Then put them in the correct order to make the completed main body text. Write an introduction and general statement to complete the essay.

1.	Both the 20–24 and the 25–29 group shared the same rate ...
2.	The first point to note is that, despite increasing almost constantly from a little under 30 live births per thousand ...
3.	Women in their early 30s, by contrast, experienced a steady increase ...
4.	However, women in their late 20s had rates consistently higher than ...

A	in 2005 to exactly 60 in 2011, the 35–39 age group always had a lower rate of birth than any other group.
B	all other groups until 2011.
C	of a little under 140 in 2005 and then followed similar downward trends.
D	in birth rate from just under 70 to just under 120 over the same time period and moved from being the third lowest to the highest group from approximately 2011 onwards.

Writing Task 1 – **Main Body** – Prepositions

Prepositions of DIRECTION

TO - pollution levels rose **to** a peak of 6 million metric tonnes in 1972

Prepositions of TIME

ON - **on** Monday

AT - **at** noon / **at** night / **at** midnight / **at** 6 o'clock / at 6 pm

IN - **in** October / **in** 2007 / **in** spring

Prepositions for PERIODS OF TIME

SINCE - sales had risen **since** 2003

FOR - exports fell **for** three consecutive years

FROM … TO - **from** 2003 **to** 2009

FROM … UNTIL - **from** 1998 **until** 2007

DURING - **during** the first half of this decade

WITHIN - sales had risen to become the highest **within** the last 10 years

Prepositions of SPATIAL RELATIONSHIPS

ABOVE - sales in Brazil were always **above** those of the other countries

BELOW - sales in Argentina were always **below** all other countries from 1996 onwards

Prepositions of POSITION

AT - remained **at** / peaked **at** / troughed **at**

IN - **in** Germany / **in** Asia / **in** all 5 European countries

OVER - sales were just **over** $65,000

UNDER - sales fell by a little **under** $27,000

Prepositions of TRANSPORT

ON - **on** foot

BY - **by** car / **by** ship / **by** train / **by** bus / **by** plane / **by** bicycle

Prepositions of AMOUNT

BY - sales fell **by** £37,000 / pollution levels rose **by** 62,500 m³

OF - Japan experienced a decrease **of** £5 million in exports

TO / FROM - sales increased **to** US$35,000 **from** US$18,000

FROM / TO - exports fell **from** £6.3 million **to** £2.7 million

Used with permission from: *IELTS – The Complete Guide to Task 1 Writing* by Phil Biggerton

Writing Task 1 – Main Body – Prepositions

Exercise
Look at the table below and complete the text that follows by adding the correct prepositions.

Task 1
The percentage of women in tertiary education in selected countries.

	1998	1999	2000	2001	2002	2003	2004	2005
Bulgaria	60.9	59.5	57.3	56.3	54.0	52.8	52.5	52.1
Denmark	55.5	56.3	56.9	56.5	57.5	57.9	57.9	57.4
Finland	53.5	54.0	53.7	53.9	54.1	53.5	53.4	53.6
Iceland	60.0	62.2	61.9	62.7	63.2	63.7	64.5	64.9
Japan	44.6	44.7	44.9	44.9	45.1	45.6	45.8	45.9
Norway	56.7	57.4	58.4	59.2	59.6	59.7	59.6	59.6
Sweden	56.2	57.6	58.2	59.1	59.5	59.6	59.6	59.6
United Kingdom	52.7	53.2	53.9	54.5	55.2	55.9	57.0	57.2
United States	55.6	52.8	55.8	55.9	56.3	56.6	57.1	57.2

The table provides statistical data **1.** _____ changes **2.** _____ the percentage **3.** _____ women in tertiary education in nine selected countries over an 8-year period from 1998 to 2005.

In general, participation **4.** _____ this level of education increased in all countries with the notable exception of Bulgaria which decreased.

More specifically, despite having the overall highest percentage in 1998 **5.** _____ 60.9% of women studying, figures in Bulgaria decreased consistently over this period ending **6.** _____ the second to last position with 52.1%. Although the percentage of students rose in Japan, from 44.6% to 45.9% over the 8 years, they remained in 9th position. Figures in Sweden remained **7.** _____ 59.6% over 3-consecutive years from 2003 to 2005 which was 3.4% higher than **8.** _____ the start of this survey. The only country to experience a continued growth was the UK where percentages grew **9.** _____ 52.7% to 57.2%; a climb of 4.5% and the second largest overall increase. This is almost certainly the result of greater competition leading to the need for more qualified employees.

Exercise
The general statement used above is a typical trend sentence. It would also be possible to use a general statement main idea like the one shown below:

In general, a greater percentage of women in Iceland were in tertiary education than in any another country whereas the lowest involvement in this level of education was in Japan.

Why could you not write: ….. more women in Iceland were in tertiary education …..?

Also, what do you think of the very last sentence in this main body? Can we add our own opinions?

Writing Task 1 – **Main Body** – Prepositions

Exercise

Look at the table taken from a survey conducted in the UK in 2009 about household chores and then try to complete the essay below it by adding prepositions.

	Cleaning	Cooking	Gardening	Shopping	Maintenance /
Males	0 hours	2 hours	5 hours	3 hours	6 hours
Females	18 hours	16 hours	3 hours	5 hours	0.5 hours

The table compares and contrasts data **1.** _____ the differences **2.** _____ the amount **3.** _____ time spent **4.** _____ both sexes, **5.** _____ an average week **6.** _____ the United Kingdom, **7.** _____ five different household activities **8.** _____ 2009.

In general, men spent most **9.** _____ their time maintaining or repairing things whereas women spent the majority of their time cleaning.

Maintenance and repairs (6 hours) was the most time-consuming household task **10.** _____ men whereas it was the least common activity **11.** _____ women; spending only 30 minutes per week **12.** _____ this. Similarly, women spent the most amount of time **13.** _____ cleaning (18 hours) but men spent none of their time. Men, **14.** _____ average, spent five hours gardening which was just **15.** _____ double the time spent **16.** _____ the same activity **17.** _____ women (3 hours). By contrast, the amount of time women spent **18.** _____ cooking (16 hours) was exactly eight times more than the time spent **19.** _____ men **20.** _____ the kitchen. One further point to note is that women spent the same amount **21.** _____ time shopping as men did gardening (5 hours).

Understanding how to use prepositions correctly will add greatly to your ability to get a higher grade in your test. Think of prepositions not as separate words, that you always need to decide where to put, but as being linked to different phrases. This saves time and also makes your grammar more accurate.

Used with permission from: *IELTS – The Complete Guide to Task 1 Writing* by Phil Biggerton

Writing Task 1 – **Main Body** – Analysing

Exercise

Look at the example Task 1 essay that follows the diagram about oil exports from Libya. Now, with a partner, decide what you like and dislike about this essay. Then, write your own essay.

Task 1

The diagram below shows information on oil exports from Libya in 2011.

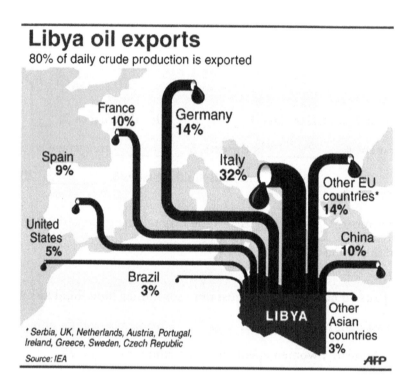

The picture below tells you about data on oil exports in 2011 from Libya.

Generally speaking, different countries have different amounts of oil from Libya in 2011.

First of all Italy has the most oil from Libya with 32% because their country is close politically to Libya. Secondly, Germany has the next biggest amount of oil with 14% which is the same as other EU countries like Serbia, UK, Netherlands, Austria, Portugal, Ireland, Greece, Sweden, Czech Republic. The France and China are next with 10% each. Spain only has roughly 9% of the oil but this is enough for them. Then United States has a little less than Spain with 5%. Finally, Brazil has only 3% of oil from Libya which is strange. Also, other Asian countries share 3% between them.

Reading- Sentence Completion

> **IELTS Tips**
>
> Look for signpost words.
>
> Answers are usually in order.

Sentence completion is simply a matter of finding a sentence in the text that contains the same information as in the question sentence. When you have found it, read both sentences and decide what information is missing. There are several things that can help with this:

1. Decide what kind of word you are looking for – verb, noun (singular/plural), adjective.
2. How many words are you looking for – did you read the instructions?
3. Look at what word comes directly before and after the missing word.

Why do you think the last idea is important? How can it help you find the answer more easily?

Signpost Words

Words directly before and/or after the missing word or words can be called signpost words. Just as a signpost shows the way to a particular place or building, signpost words often show where the answer is in the text.

It works like this. Remember that the two sentences – the question sentence and text sentence – contain the same information. Although it is possible that the text sentence contains more information than the question sentence, one sentence is basically a paraphrased version of the other.

If you have already studied the sections on Task 1 Writing introductions, you will know that sentences can be changed by using synonyms and rearranging information. If you do this correctly, you end up with an introduction that is more formal in style but – apart from any additional information you might have added – is essentially the same sentence. Let's take a simple question sentence example:

1. XTC stopped touring in ……….. because of Andy Partridge's stage fright.

The signpost words in this example are 'in' and 'because'. These are next to the missing information.

This might be seen in the text as:

In 1982 Andy Partridge's stage fright resulted in the cancellation of the XTC tour.

You should have realised that the answer is probably a place, or month or year (possibly a season). There are several keywords you could have chosen – **XTC, Andy Partridge's, stage fright**. When you find these keywords in the text then you are probably looking at the sentence that contains the answer.

Read the text sentence carefully and try to find what information is missing from the question sentence. If you are still not sure then maybe signpost words can help you. One of the signpost words in this example is '**in**'. It is still in the original text sentence and points to the answer – the word next to it – 1982.

NOTE: There is another '**in**' in the text sentence but this introduces the phrase – '**the cancellation**' – which does not fit the kind of answer you are looking for.

Although it is easy to paraphrase certain words and phrases, some words are more difficult. Think of the preposition "in" seen in the example above and others like it such as: **for, to, on, by**. Very often these words remain unchanged and stay next to the word or words you are looking for. The more you look for signpost words the more they will help you when completing sentences, tables and summaries.

Ailing Musicians

Musicians experience a range of maladies, including carpal tunnel syndrome, musculoskeletal complaints and allergic reactions.

In 1974, the 'BMJ' published a brief report of a delicate medical complaint afflicting regular players of the cello, dubbed cello scrotum. Sadly, it was a spoof. Baroness Murphy (Dr Elaine Murphy) owned up in 2009 when other papers started referencing the original study.

While cello scrotum may be fiction, there are many real conditions affecting musicians. Not surprisingly, hearing damage is an occupational hazard not just to those in rock bands but also classical performers situated close to loud instruments such as trombones.

The repeated movements many players have to make leave them at risk of repetitive strain injury (RSI). Guitarists, for example, are prone to carpal tunnel syndrome, when bones in the wrist begin to press on nerves as they pass through a channel (the carpal tunnel). Numbness, pins and needles, and pain can all ensue. Jonny Greenwood, guitarist with Radiohead, plays with a splint on his right wrist because of RSI.

The unusual posture needed to play many instruments can predispose to a variety of musculoskeletal complaints, leading to back pain or other local discomfort. Another common problem is spontaneous muscle contraction (focal dystonia), particularly in the fingers.

Allergic reactions or other skin disorders may arise where skin comes into contact with an instrument. These lead to instrument-specific conditions, such as 'fiddler's neck', 'flautist's chin' and 'guitar nipple'.

Brass players are at risk of abnormalities affecting their 'embouchure' (the complex arrangement of lips and other tissues at instruments' mouthpieces). Legendary jazz musician Louis Armstrong suffered particularly badly because of his forceful playing style. The condition is known as 'Satchmo syndrome' in his honour.

Sometimes instrument playing can reveal underlying health problems. A 17-year-old trumpet player suffered transient ischaemic episodes ('mini-strokes') when playing, later found to be caused by a hole in his heart. Surgery corrected the heart defect and cured his symptoms.

Female musicians tend to be affected slightly more often than men, and string players more often than percussionists. Rest is the most common therapy and generally resolves musculoskeletal complaints. Involuntary muscle contractions are very difficult to treat and can end musical careers.

Like all performers, musicians can suffer performance anxiety about playing in public. At its worst, extreme stage fright can potentially end professional careers. Barbra Streisand did not perform in public for nearly 30 years because of stage fright, which may also have affected the brilliant but eccentric classical pianist Glenn Gould. XTC stopped touring in 1982 because of Andy Partridge's stage fright. Fortunately, a variety of psychotherapies are available for people with 'performance anxiety'.

Rock and pop

In popular music, touring can be hazardous to health. Falling from the stage has injured several performers, including Ryan Adams and Jim James of My Morning Jacket. Stage diving or crowd surfing is a dangerous pastime (Jamie Reynolds of the Klaxons broke his leg doing it in 2007, while Mike Skinner of The Streets aggravated an old hernia in Cambridge in January 2009). Some performers run the risk of being pelted with objects such as bottles (or, in David Bowie's case, a lollipop).

More seriously, the 'rock and roll lifestyle' has claimed numerous lives, particularly due to drug overdose or the long-term effects of overindulgence. A recent study of more than 1,000 rock and pop stars found that even after their period of fame, they had a substantially higher risk of dying than matched controls.

Perhaps the most unusual case, though, is the fate of country singer Johnny Cash. In 1983, he was kicked in the stomach by an ostrich. Unfortunately, a severe abdominal injury led to a dependence on pain-killers and a descent into addiction.

Questions 1–7

Complete the sentences.

*Choose **NO MORE THAN THREE WORDS** from the passage for each answer.*

1. Repetitive strain injury is the result of ...the repeated movements.
2. Many problems with muscles and the skeleton are due to a musician's unusual postures
3. One medical condition named after a famous musician was ...Satchmo Syndrome.
4. ......men..... tend to be less affected than ...female musicians
5. Stage fright might have affected the career of ....professional
6. A musician broke his leg when he was .....stage diving/crowd surfing
7. Retired rock stars have a higher chance of ...dying..... than controls.

Reading– Matching – Sentence Completion

Overcoming Culture Shock

After arriving at your new university or college, the following suggestions may assist you in reducing the strain of culture shock.

Read a local newspaper and find out what the topical issues are. If you are well informed, you can hold conversations with British people without always feeling the outsider.

If you are unsure of your English, boost your confidence by remembering that most British people do not speak a foreign language. Make an effort at improving your language skills by watching TV and listening to the radio. Your institution may run free courses for international students.

Take a break from studying and take part in social activities. Enquire about things like etiquette and dress code if you are at all unsure.

Ask questions about social customs from people with whom you feel comfortable. You will always find someone who will assist you in finding out about life in Britain. This can be a two-way exchange, with you telling people about life in your home country.

Keep in touch with your own culture. The university's International Welfare Officer should know, for instance, where the nearest temples and mosques are and where you can buy the cooking ingredients that you are used to from home.

Help to reduce stress on your body by keeping fit physically.

If you are feeling very low, talk to someone about it. This could be your fellow students, your landlord, or university staff such as the International Welfare Officer or Student Counsellor.

Write down things you like and do not like. Can you change them? If not, perhaps you can find a way of living with them.

And finally, remember that other students probably go through the same experiences as you do. Even British students have to adjust to living away from home.

Questions 1– 4

Complete the sentences by choosing a correct phrase. An example has been done for you.

Example: If you are well read, __B__ with British people.	A you can talk to yourself
	B you can have in-depth discussions
1. Your school might offer free lessons ____E____.	C by exercising
2. Ask about ____D____.	D for international institutions
3. Cut down body stress ____C____.	E for overseas students
4. Should you feel down ____G____.	F other students will too
	G converse with somebody
	H the way people behave and the clothes they wear

Writing Task 1– Pie Chart

Task 1.
The chart below shows how the average family in the USA spends their money.

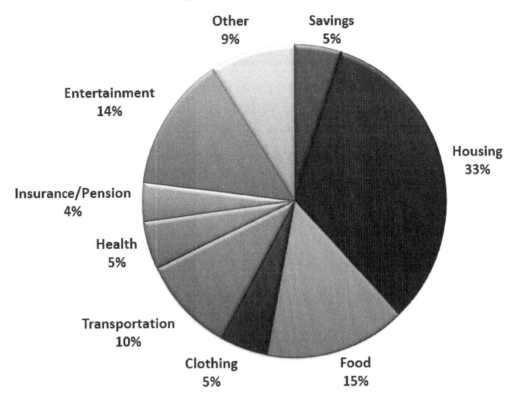

Exercise
Complete the text below by adding the correct prepositions.

The pie chart provides data **1.** _____ how a typical family **2.** _____ America spends their money **3.** _____ nine different categories.

In general, the biggest portion **4.** _____ their budget goes **5.** _____ housing whereas the least amount **6.** _____ money is spent **7.** _____ insurance and pension plans.

More specifically, almost exactly one-third (33%) of a family's total budget goes **8.** _____ their accommodation. This is contrasted **9.** _____ the 4% that is allotted **10.** _____ insurance or pensions. Exactly 5% of the total income was spent on each of three categories clothing, health, and savings. The 15% spent **11.** _____ food makes it the second largest expense and is closely followed by entertainment **12.** _____ a slightly lower amount of 14%. The amount given to other overheads is 9% and so slightly less than the 10% spent on transportation. The three largest financial commitments **13.** _____ a family, that is housing, food, and entertainment, total almost two-thirds **14.** _____ the total budget at 62%.

Writing Task 1 – IELTS Tips

INTRODUCTIONS

The two biggest problems are:

COPYING – most students understand that they must not copy the Task 1 introduction but the examiner will still see it as a problem even if you include small sections from the Task 1 introduction.

NOT WRITING ENOUGH INFORMATION – this may take the form of either leaving out information already provided in the Task 1 introduction or not finding all of the extra information from the chart. Remember to always include, time, time period, number of items **AND** look for the units. You don't have to put the units in the introduction (although you can) but check for units when you first look at the chart because you might forget later.

GENERAL STATEMENTS can focus on the overall trend, or main idea, if the chart has a time period/age groups but when writing about a chart with no time period you can mention what the biggest and smallest items are. Do NOT add figures from the main body in the general statement.

In the **MAIN BODY** we **NEVER** put a number before the word *percentage*. We have to use the word *per cent* or use the symbol %. *The money spent on advertising on television (US$3,000,000) makes up ___ per cent of the total advertising budget.*

However, we can use the word *percentage* when no figures are written before it. *The biggest percentage of the budget was spent on advertising on television and made up ___ per cent of the total expenditure.* We can also use *percentage* when we are writing about charts where the numbers we are looking at change over a period of time.

Also, we never put 's' after a number. *Production of air conditioners in South Africa increased to 15 millions in 2006.* The units are often shown to be in *millions, thousands* and *hundreds* but you must **NOT** use 's' when you use numbers.

Writing Task 1 – Flow Charts

A lot of students think that studying bar charts, lines charts, tables, and pie charts is enough. However, if you stop here you have a good chance of seeing a diagram in your test that you have never studied. This is a good way to get a low grade in your writing test.

What do processes, flow charts and cycles have in common? Think about the following examples and think about what might connect them in some way.

> **A process** – *the production of chocolate*
> **A flow chart** – *designing artwork for a customer*
> **A cycle** – *the butterfly lifecycle*

If we think about them more carefully, we can see that time is a factor in all of them. They all happen over a period of time and can be divided into stages or steps. For example, look at the flow chart concerning the designing of graphics from a customer's artwork.

Task 1
The diagram below shows how artwork is turned into graphics.

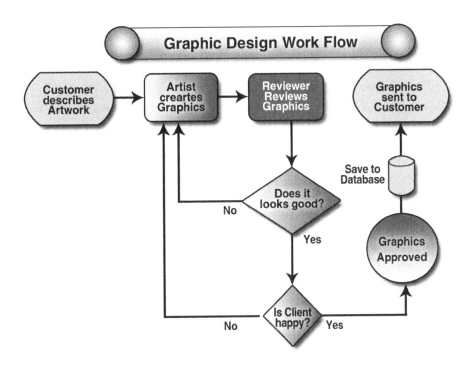

The preparation needed before you start writing involves reading everything carefully (both the instructions and everything in the diagram), and deciding the sequence of each stage. It is a good idea to write the number of each stage on the diagram so that when you start writing you simply work through the numbers. Unlike other Task 1 diagrams that we have already seen, this is a very descriptive style of writing and does not require any analysis of numbers.

Exercise
Try to write the introduction and main body. No general statement is needed for flow charts, processes and cycles. Although a conclusion is not needed, one can be written if you finish the first two paragraphs and find that you haven't written enough.

Writing Task 1 – **Flow Charts** – Simple Passive

The simple present passive is often used when writing about a flow chart.

Exercise
Look at the text below written about the flow chart on page 39 and underline all of the passive verbs. Has the passive been used for all of the verbs? Is the simple present passive the only passive form used here?

> The illustration details the various stages involved in the creation of graphics from a customer's description of his artwork.
>
> First of all, the customer talks to the graphic artist about his artwork and describes what he wants. The artist then creates the graphics using the information that he has been given. The finished graphics are subsequently reviewed by a reviewer to see how good they are. After this, if it is felt that they do not look very good, they go back to the graphic artist who redesigns them. If, however, the graphics pass the standards set by the company, they are passed to the client who will either approve or reject them. If they are considered unacceptable they go back to the designer. However, if the graphics are to the client's liking, they will be approved and saved in their database. Once the graphics have been stored in the company's data base, they are sent to the customer.

Exercise
Read the text again and notice how time order phrases like "First of all," "then," and "subsequently" are used to create a more coherent flow of information. Notice that no general statement was used in the text about designing graphics and is usually not written for any flow chart, process, or cycle.

The reason for using the simple present passive form of verbs when possible is that this is seen as being more academic. We do not have to do this when writing about bar charts, line charts, tables and pie charts but we do have this option when writing about flow charts, processes and cycles. The main difference is that the passive is used to move the focus away from the person or thing doing the action to the thing receiving the action. This is commonly seen in university level writing.

Exercise
Complete the sentences by turning the verbs in brackets into the simple present passive. Be careful because not all verbs follow the formula: **is/are + verb/ed**.

1. The corn, once fully mature, _____ (harvest)

2. The water _____ (boil) and then the tea _____ (add)

3. The sieve _____ (shake) in order to remove the dirt.

4. The trees _____ (cut) before _____ (transport) to the wood mill.

5. Subsequently, an e-mail is _____ (write) and then sent to the company.

Writing Task 1 – Flow Chart – Test Practice

Exercise

Look at the diagram below and write a complete essay – introduction, main body (and conclusion if needed).

Task 1

You should spend about 20 minutes on this task.

The chart below shows how an application letter is either accepted or rejected.

Summarise the information by selecting and reporting the main features, and make comparisons where relevant.

Write at least 150 words.

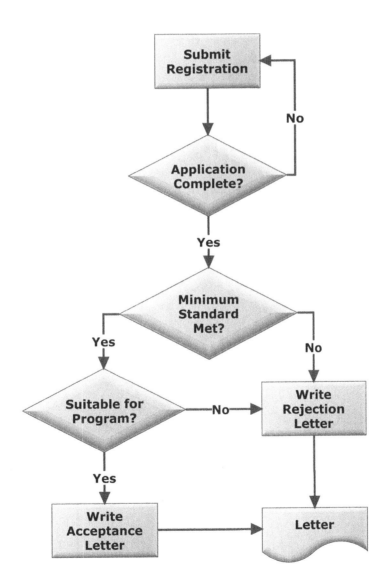

Map – Test Practice You should spend about 20 minutes on this task.

The diagrams below show how Boracay Island has grown as a tourist destination from 1970 to 2010.

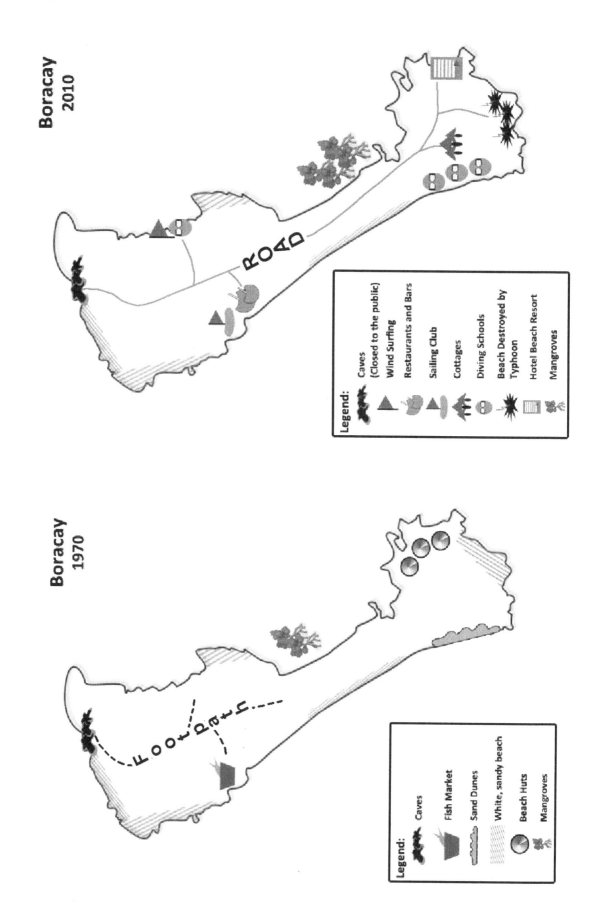

Reading – Summary Completion

Summaries can be seen as an extension of the sentence completion question type and so the skills needed to complete either skill are exactly the same.

There are two types of summary:

- ♦ Complete sentences/notes by using words taken from the text.
- ♦ Complete sentences/notes by using the list of words provided in a box.

Answers from the text

If you have to find the answers from the text then treat each sentence/note as you would if it was a sentence completion question type. Pick a good keyword and then find the sentence in the text that matches the information in the question – use signpost words if you can to help – then find the word or words (read the instructions) that are needed to complete the question sentence/note.

Answers from a box

If you have to find the answer from a list then the process is the same as if you are finding the words from the text. Find what information is missing but then look at the list of words and see which word best fits. The word you choose from the list might be the same as the word you selected from the text but it could be different.

Common ways to confuse students are by changing the order of the information given in the text. This can mean that a sentence in the text saying – **The population of Tokyo is greater than that of London** – could be rewritten in the summary as – **London has a ……….. population than Tokyo**. The list of possible words to choose from could contain the words – **greater** – **smaller** – but if you are tempted to use the word – **greater** – as the answer think again. Of course, the answer is not – **greater** – you would have to use the word – **smaller**.

Another way to confuse you can be by using a different form of the word. For instance, if the text sentence says – **The full moon is a time when many villagers like to fish** – but the summary states – **The villagers like to go ……….. whenever there is a full moon**. The list of words might contain the words – **fishing** – **fish** – if you picked – **fish** – think again!

Finally, a synonym might be used to replace the word from the text. This will really test your vocabulary range and is yet another reason to start to build on what words you already know.

Reading – Summary Completion

An Era of Abundance

Our knowledge of the complex pathways underlying digestive processes is rapidly expanding, although there is still a great deal we do not fully understand. On the one hand, digestion, like any other major human biological system, is astonishing in its intricacy and cleverness. Our bodies manage to extract the complex resources needed to survive, despite sharply varying conditions, while at the same time, filtering out a multiplicity of toxins.

On the other hand, our bodies evolved in a very different era. Our digestive processes in particular are optimized for a situation that is dramatically dissimilar to the one we find ourselves in. For most of our biological heritage, there was a high likelihood that the next foraging or hunting season (and for a brief, relatively recent period, the next planting season) might be catastrophically lean. So it made sense for our bodies to hold on to every possible calorie. Today, this biological strategy is extremely counterproductive. Our outdated metabolic programming underlies our contemporary epidemic of obesity and fuels pathological processes of degenerative disease such as coronary artery disease, and type II diabetes.

Up until recently (on an evolutionary time scale), it was not in the interest of the species for old people like myself (I was born in 1948) to use up the limited resources of the clan. Evolution favored a short life span – life expectancy was 37 years only two centuries ago – so these restricted reserves could be devoted to the young, those caring for them, and laborers strong enough to perform intense physical work.

We now live in an era of great material abundance. Most work requires mental effort rather than physical exertion. A century ago, 30 percent of the U.S. work force worked on farms, with another 30 percent deployed in factories. Both of these figures are now under 3 percent. The significant majority of today's job categories, ranging from airline flight attendant to web designer, simply didn't exist a century ago.

Our species has already augmented the "natural" order of our life cycle through our technology: drugs, supplements, replacement parts for virtually all bodily systems, and many other interventions. We already have devices to replace our hips, knees, shoulders, elbows, wrists, jaws, teeth, skin, arteries, veins, heart valves, arms, legs, feet, fingers, and toes. Systems to replace more complex organs (for example, our hearts) are beginning to work. As we're learning the principles of operation of the human body and the brain, we will soon be in a position to design vastly superior systems that will be more enjoyable, last longer, and perform better, without susceptibility to breakdown, disease, and aging.

In a famous scene from the movie, *The Graduate*, Benjamin's mentor gives him career advice in a single word: "plastics." Today, that word might be "software," or "biotechnology," but in another couple of decades, the word is likely to be "nanobots." Nanobots – blood-cell-sized robots – will provide the means to radically redesign our digestive systems, and, incidentally, just about everything else.

In an intermediate phase, nanobots in the digestive tract and bloodstream will intelligently extract the precise nutrients we need, call for needed additional nutrients and supplements through our personal wireless local area network, and send the rest of the food we eat on its way to be passed through for elimination.

If this seems futuristic, keep in mind that intelligent machines are already making their way into our blood stream. There are dozens of projects underway to create blood-stream-based "biological microelectromechanical systems" (bioMEMS) with a wide range of diagnostic and therapeutic applications. BioMEMS devices are being designed to intelligently scout out pathogens and deliver medications in very precise ways.

For example, a researcher at the University of Illinois at Chicago has created a tiny capsule with pores measuring only seven nanometers. The pores let insulin out in a controlled manner but prevent antibodies from invading the pancreatic Islet cells inside the capsule. These nanoengineered devices have cured rats with type I diabetes, and there is no reason that the same methodology would fail to work in humans. Similar systems could precisely deliver dopamine to the brain for Parkinson's patients, provide blood-clotting factors for patients with hemophilia, and deliver cancer drugs directly to tumor sites. A new design provides up to 20 substance-containing reservoirs that can release their cargo at programmed times and locations in the body. A new world is on the horizon and you will be part of it.

Questions 1–8

Complete the summary below.

*Choose **NO MORE THAN THREE WORDS** from the passage for each answer.*

In the past it was essential to hoard our calories for as long as possible because our food source was mainly restricted to **1.** _foraging_ and **2.** _hunting_ which brought in irregular supplies. However, these reserves were intended for **3.** _survival_ because they had the power and energy to work hard. Nowadays, the focus has moved away from jobs on **4.** _farms_ and in **5.** _factories_ to jobs that weren't available **6.** _a century ago_. Through technology, it has now become possible to replace many body **7.** _parts_ and as techniques improve we will be able to develop better **8.** _life cycle_ ✗

Questions 9–12

*Complete the summary using the list of words, **A–J**, below.*

In the future, a nanobot's ability to redesign our digestive system will be **9.** _____ E _____ . One function is the intelligent **10.** _____ I _____ of the exact nutritional requirements needed. If this all seems to be fantasy, consider a tiny machine already developed that has now been used in the treatment of **11.** _____ ✗ F _____ . However, this has not been tried on **12.** _____ D _____ .

A Parkinson's	B haemophilia	C diabetes	D humans	E radical
F rats	G extract	H radically	I extraction	J cells

Reading – Summary Completion

The History of Thai Food

Thai food is famous all over the world. Whether chili-hot or comparatively bland, harmony and contrast are the guiding principles behind each dish. Thai cuisine is essentially a marriage of centuries-old Eastern and Western influences harmoniously combined into something uniquely Thai. Characteristics of Thai food depend on who cooks it and where it is cooked. Dishes can be refined and adjusted to suit all tastes.

Originally, Thai cooking reflected the characteristics of a waterborne lifestyle. Aquatic animals, plant and herbs were major ingredients. With their Buddhist background, Thais shunned the use of large pieces of meat. Big cuts of meat were shredded and blended with herbs and spices. Traditional Thai cooking methods were stewing and baking, or grilling but Chinese influences saw the introduction of frying, stir-frying and deep-frying. Chilies and other ingredients were introduced to Thai cooking by Portuguese missionaries who had acquired a taste for South American culinary ingredients while working there during the late 1600s. Culinary influences from the 17th century onwards included Portuguese, Dutch, French and Japanese techniques. Thais were very adept at adapting foreign cooking methods, and substituting ingredients. The ghee used in Indian cooking was replaced with coconut oil, and coconut milk substituted for other dairy products.

Overpowering pure spices were toned down and enhanced by fresh herbs such as lemon grass and galangal. Eventually, fewer and less spices were used in Thai curries, while the use of fresh herbs increased. It is generally acknowledged that Thai curries burn intensely, but briefly, whereas other curries, with strong spices, burn for longer periods. Instead of serving dishes in courses, a Thai meal is served all at once, permitting diners to enjoy complementary combinations of different tastes.

Questions 1–10

Complete the summary below.

*Choose **NO MORE THAN TWO WORDS** from the passage for each answer.*

Although the main tenets of every meal are **1.** _harmony_ and **2.** _contrast_, the final taste is determined by who cooks it. At first, the ingredients used in Thai cooking were the result of a **3.** _waterborne_ way of life. Cooking techniques became more varied thanks to the **4.** _foreign cooking methods_. Thai ingredients started to become more eclectic with the introduction of products from South America such as **5.** _Chillies_. Further change began in the 17th century through the influence of people from various countries such as the **6.** _Portuguese_ and **7.** _Japanese_ and the substitution of **8.** _ghee_ with **9.** _Coconut oil_. One main difference between Thai curries and those from other countries is that the latter burn for **10.** _intensely / briefly_.

Writing Task 2 – Topics

As you begin to study Task 2 writing you will begin to learn new skills that are different to the main focus of a Task 1 essay. You must still be careful with grammar, spelling and the use of appropriate vocabulary, but other skills also need to be practised and improved. Perhaps the biggest problem for students to overcome is knowing how to develop the topic given to them. This is a very important skill because the final grade given to you by the examiner is based on not only grammatical and structural awareness but also the actual content of your essay. This means that you might be able to show good writing skills but the information given might be very weak. As you continue to work through this book you will see that we can divide the ability to write into two main parts:

Presentation can be seen as how the words, sentences and paragraphs connect to produce a well structured piece of writing. One sentence should flow smoothly into the next, and paragraphs placed in a logical, progressive style. This is often referred to as cohesion. In some ways you can regard all of this as the framework on which to add your information – the reason for you writing the essay.

Content is, in terms of the IELTS test, the development of your ideas and opinions in a logical, progressive style. Information and ideas that have not been developed will result in a lower grade being given.

Exercise
Discover some of the most common topics used in the Task 2 writing test by completing the crossword. Use the definitions of each word at the bottom of this page to help. You can use a dictionary to help.

ACROSS
1. The community in which a person lives.
2. The characteristics of a group of people that makes them unique.
3. Your surroundings, especially natural surroundings.
4. The process of learning different things.
5. The study of the environment.

DOWN
1. The state of a living body.
2. The practical application of knowledge.
3. The economic activity related to serving people when they travel.
4. When the local or national ways of doing things becomes international.

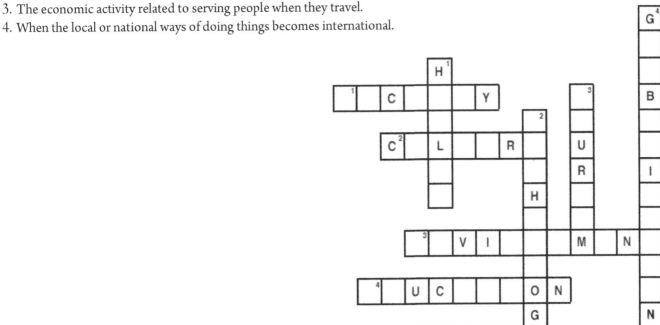

Writing Task 2 – Understanding the Topic

Recognizing the topic is not so difficult but knowing how to approach the essay can be more complicated. Luckily, there are only three main essay types, but it is essential to become very familiar with all three and the different ways you are told what to do. Be careful: if the wrong essay is written a lower grade will automatically be given.

The three types are:

> **A**   Agree or disagree with a stated opinion
>
> **B**   Present advantages and disadvantages of a stated situation / issue
>
> **C**   Provide possible effects and solutions to a particular problem

Exercise

Look at some typical Task 2 instructions seen in the IELTS test and decide which essay type they are: **A**, **B** or **C**.

1.   What do you think are the effects of global warming? What solutions can you suggest?

2.   Many are of the opinion that television is an important medium for imparting useful information. Others, however, disagree and think that more control over what young people see should be imposed. To what extent do you agree or disagree?

3.   What are the advantages and disadvantages of having a gap year?

Notice that some instructions are inferred. That is to say, if the Task 2 statement is an opinion but no instructions follow, the essay type is Agree/Disagree. For instance:

> Many Western countries are facing a serious decrease in population levels which will seriously affect their economy in the future. Governments should, therefore, offer incentives to encourage couples to have more children.

This type of essay is sometimes mistaken for a problem/solution essay but the difference here is that one solution to declining population figures has already been given as an opinion. This opinion becomes the focus of the essay and you must agree or disagree with it. You are not asked to offer alternative solutions.

It is better to focus on one side of the argument rather than be somewhere in the middle. Even experienced writers can end up arguing against themselves if they decide to sit on the fence. There, 100% agree or 100% disagree and confirm this in the introduction by stating that, for instance, 'I completely agree that ....'

Writing Task 2 – **Presentation** – Essay Outline

To look at the basic outline of a Task 2 essay we need to decide how many paragraphs need to be written. Although there are a number of different possibilities, an ideal number to use would be four paragraphs as this format suits the three types of essay you need to study.

This approach to writing may seem rather restrictive and can be seen as limiting the students' ability to express themselves in a more creative way. However, for an IELTS student, who often has limited time to develop the necessary skills to achieve a high score, this is perfect. Each paragraph contains a specific type of information and so both structure and content can be written in a more effective and controlled manner. Showing the IELTS examiner that you understand the structure of an essay and know what needs to go where is a very important part of getting a better grade.

Remember: Academic writing values accuracy over creativity and does not value an individual style of writing over the tried and tested formal style used at university.

Exercise
Match the sample sentences below with the introduction, main body or conclusion and decide which type of essay they are probably from. Write:

> **A** ..... if it is Agree / Disagree
> **B** ..... if it is Advantage / Disadvantage
> **C** ..... if it is Problem / Solution

1. As a result, more attention has been paid to the benefits and drawbacks of developing zoos as a means to protect them.

2. In conclusion, although there are obvious drawbacks to studying overseas there are clearly more benefits.

3. The government should begin to develop better methods of controlling the damage brought about by large increases in tourism.

4. Finally, the chance to learn social skills with both sexes also helps strengthen my conviction that mixed schools are the preferred environment for students.

5. Despite overwhelming evidence to the contrary, many people still feel that capital punishment is an effective way of reducing the number of offenders.

How many sentences do you think you need to write a 250-word essay?

The exact structure of your essay will depend on the instructions given to you. These instructions must be followed closely or you risk ending with a lower grade than you deserve. Typically you will read:

Agree - Disagree Essay Do you agree or disagree? / Discuss both sides and then give your opinion.

Advantage - Disadvantage Essay Discuss the advantages and disadvantages of this and then give your own opinion. / Do you think the advantages outweigh the disadvantages?

Problem - Solution Essay What are the problems associated with this, and what are some of the solutions?

Writing Task 2 – **Presentation** – Informal vs. Formal

Writing can be divided into two main writing styles - informal and formal. Both are seen as correct styles of English but are used in different situations. Informal writing is typically used for such things as emails, letters to friends, and memos whereas formal writing is used for business letters, reports, and academic papers. When writing the Task 2 essay, you need to use the formal style.

Certain generalizations can be made to help you develop a more formal style and these need to be followed for both Task 1 and Task 2. This will benefit you when you study at university because your professor will not accept essays that are informal and non-academic in style.

1.	Do not use common (often clichéd) expressions. Informal Formal **kids** ………………….... children **bucks** ………………….... money **kind of / sort of** …………. somewhat / rather **first** ………………….... firstly **on the other hand** ……….. conversely / by contrast **really** …………………... very
2.	Try to avoid direct (or indirect) references to people as much as possible Avoid using **"one"** For instance: **One finds that** … can change into … **It can be found that** …
3.	Do not use contractions like … **haven't** … **should've** … **can't**
4.	Use complete words … **August** … **television** … **United States** … not … **Aug** … **TV**… **US** unless the abbreviation is commonly used and are almost never written in full … **NATO, WHO, BMW**
5.	When a number starts a sentence write the word … **"Three thousand two hundred and fifty seven people celebrated the Mayor of London's wedding."** Write numbers for one and two words … **five** … **eight** … **one thousand** Use numerals for three or more words … **196** … **2,589** … **67.3**
6.	Do not ask questions or use exclamation marks or ampersands … **?** … **!** … **&**
7.	Do not use common abbreviations … **e.g.** … **i.e.** … **etc.**
8.	Do not use coordinating conjunctions to start sentences … **and** … **but** … **so** … **or**
9.	Do not use idioms or proverbs … **"Every coin has two sides"**
10.	Do not use imperatives for giving suggestions, advice or instructions … **Sit down** … **Stand up** … **Be quiet**

Exercise
Use the 10 tips in the box above to alter the informal paragraph below about Global Warming.

> *Do you think global warming is a big problem? Although it is difficult for me to do anything about this, many countries like the U.S. and the U.K. are making rules to help, e.g. monitoring carbon dioxide emissions more carefully. And more and more countries are beginning to encourage people to use public transport. Changes take time but many hands make light work.*

Writing Task 2 – **Informal vs. Formal** – Essay Outline

Although the writing style you need to learn for both Task 1 and Task 2 writing is formal, it does not really reach the level of formality needed in a more academic setting. However, this book will certainly help you develop a more acceptable style when you start studying at university.

Exercise
Look at the sentences below and decide which words, phrases or even sentences are too informal. Discuss your thoughts with a classmate and then change each sentence to make it more academic in style.

1. It is indisputable that most scientists see a direct link between carbon dioxide and global warming.
2. It's possible to reduce inner city pollution by encouraging car owners to use public transport.
3. Why doesn't the government try harder to solve this problem?
4. The first advantage is that speaking another language allows you to travel more easily in a foreign country.
5. Let us consider how we can encourage better relationships between countries.
6. In our daily lives we are influenced by a number of factors.
7. We, Japanese, do things in our own way.
8. We can do many things to help poor people.
9. 10 kids were given money to study at a private school because they were good students.

Exercise
Look at the table below. Match the informal verb with the formal verb, change it into a noun, and complete the sentences below with these nouns.

	Informal	Formal	Noun
1.	to help	to prevent	**Example:** prevention
2.	to give	to discover	
3.	to stop	to assist	
4.	to find	to provide	

1. .... from the government is necessary if we are to help reduce the poverty gap.
2. The .... of penicillin led to the effective treatment of diphtheria.
3. The .... of private medical insurance is an excellent company benefit.
4. The .... of further damage was made possible by an efficient fire fighting team.

Writing Task 2 – **Formal** – Academic Style

Academic writing is often seen as a style of writing that is exclusive to universities and need not be thought about until you are there. Think again!

Even native speakers are often unprepared for university life and the demands of writing research papers and reports for their professors. A good knowledge of grammar, an ability to spell correctly and a wide vocabulary range is not enough.

The typical essays written at school do not develop the necessary skills to write in a more academic style. In fact, they often encourage habits that are completely opposite to what is expected at university. A quick look at most university websites in the United Kingdom will show you that they also recognize this as a problem because they often provide information on how to write research papers, abstracts, literature reviews, methodology reports and so on.

Exercise

What do you imagine when you think of academic writing? Look at the list of definitions **(1–9)** of important factors associated with academic writing. Then, pick one word from each pair that fits each definition.

1. Characterized by deep thought – conversational / serious

2. Definitely or strictly stated, defined, or fixed – precise / vague

3. A method of studying the nature of something – analytical / impressionistic

4. Having its source in or being guided by the intellect – polemical / rational

5. Without reference or connection to a particular person – impersonal / personal

6. Evasively worded in order to avoid an unqualified statement – absolute / hedged

7. Demonstrating a high degree of mental capacity – emotional / intellectual

8. Not influenced by personal feelings, interpretations or prejudices – objective / subjective

9. Observant of conventional requirements of behavior, procedure, and so on – colloquial / formal

As you study Task 2 writing, this book will not only explain in detail how to write a good 250-word essay but also offer some insights into university style academic writing and many of the functions like analyzing, arguing, comparing, contrasting, defining, describing, explaining and evaluating that will be used when you reach university.

Exercise

Look at the short text below and try to think of ways to make it more academic.

> These days in Afghanistan a lot of guys don't have jobs. Years ago, it was normal to work on the family farm with their brothers and sisters. Why is this? One thing is that loads of people have moved to the cities because of money problems. Is this good for society? Jones has studied this and says that small farming communities will become smaller and traditions will disappear, etc. I think that he's right. Maybe they could ask the government to help by giving money to farmers.

Writing Task 2 – **Brainstorming** – Developing Your Ideas

Brainstorming is a way to maximize the ability to generate new ideas and is commonly used in groups to develop ideas more creatively and effectively. Many different techniques can be used to encourage you to become more creative in your thinking. However, it's also possible to brainstorm on your own and develop a wide range of ideas for each topic.

These skills are not about trying to remember things that seem long forgotten but are ways to stimulate your mind to think "outside of the box".

Exercise
Look at the techniques suggested below and work with a partner to decide which essay types they would be useful for. More than one answer might be possible for each technique.

1.	**Role Switching**	Imagine that you are a different person, for instance: – your mother / father – your teacher / professor – the president of your country How would they develop a topic?
2.	**Spider Mapping**	Effective spider mapping occurs when you have a clear goal, specific topic or concept to brainstorm. Use the spider map on page 100 to help develop your ideas. Draw lines from the central idea. One idea becomes one main branch and leads to other related ideas on the same branch. One map can have many branches as you continue to develop other related themes or connected ideas.
3.	**Resourcing**	Imagine a situation where resources are no longer limited. For example, limitless money, electricity, natural resources and so on. How would this change your thinking? What would limitless resources let you do that was impossible before?

Exercise
Now try these techniques when developing the topic questions given at the end of this page. Every mind works differently and so you might find that some techniques are more powerful than others.

Remember: Skills like these are very useful to practice as you will find they will help you in many situations throughout your life and not just for the IELTS test.

THINK - CREATE - DEVELOP

1. Crime in cities continues to be a problem. What are the reasons for this.? What problems might this cause?

2. Discuss the advantages and disadvantages of the continued logging of tropical rainforests.

Writing Task 2 – **Brainstorming** – Developing Your Ideas

Many IELTS students find writing about or discussing environmental problems difficult. Of course, you can read about these issues in your own language and then make notes in English. Another idea is to choose a topic and then 'brainstorm' for ideas.

Exercise
Look at the examples below and then develop other ideas both for and against the issues.

<u>**Topic:**</u> *Genetically modified crops*

FOR	AGAINST
insect-resistant crops	not safe for humans
_____	_____
_____	_____

<u>**Topic:**</u> *Cars need to be banned from inner-city areas*

FOR	AGAINST
more green areas	police cars / ambulances have limited access
_____	_____
_____	_____

Exercise
Look at the various problems listed in the box below and try to decide possible connections to the environment.

Do you	Why?
1. find the weather much warmer?	**For Example** Greenhouse Effect / too much CO_2 in the atmosphere
2. use recycled paper?	
3. shower instead of have a bath?	
4. walk short distances?	
5. take a shopping bag to the supermarket?	
6. refuse to wear certain clothes or shoes?	
7. car pool?	
8. sort your rubbish into different bags?	

Reading – Matching – Statements

IELTS Tips

Answer all the questions. If you are not sure – guess.

Answers are NOT always in order.

Why can't we live for ever?

The only certainties in life, said Benjamin Franklin, are death and taxes. Don't expect either to disappear anytime soon. The prospects for a longer life currently seem rosy, at least if you are a laboratory mouse. This year has seen headlines about mice, engineered to produce lots of antioxidants, who can live 20 per cent longer than usual, and equally impressive gains for animals altered to produce high levels of a peptide hormone known as Klotho (after the minor Greek deity). Ultra-low-calorie diets, big doses of vitamin E, and even transferring ovaries from a younger mouse into elderly females also seem to extend lifespan. Shepherds may say that sheep are just looking for new ways to die, but mice seem to be susceptible to almost anything that can make them live a bit longer.

So what are the prospects for a rather larger mammal that normally lives 70-80 years, rather than the mouse's two, and very occasionally makes it to 120 before keeling over? Will what works in mice work in humans?

There are well-publicised optimists who think it will. The most often quoted is Aubrey de Grey of Cambridge, proponent of a big expansion of research on what he has called Strategies for Engineered Negligible Senescence. He is also one of the leading lights of the Methuselah Mouse Prize, which is offered to the scientific team that develops the longest-lived mouse.

But for all his energy and revolutionary zeal, Professor de Grey is not actually doing the research - his day job is as a computer expert in a genetics lab. And many researchers in biogerontology are sceptical about his predictions. That scepticism came through recently when Tom Kirkwood of the University of Newcastle's Institute for Ageing and Health asked in Nature: "Why must advocates of life extension make preposterous claims about imminent longevity gains if they are to gain public notice?"

Professor Kirkwood is the author of the influential 'disposable soma' theory of ageing that states the body decays because there is little genetic interest in keeping it going beyond reproductive age. This means that he sees no programmed limit to lifespan, in mice or people. Ageing is a biological sin of omission, not commission. So perhaps we could block whatever is doing the damage. But, he stresses, "this does not imply that major increases in lifespan are imminent. As we grow older the accumulated burden of molecular and cellular damage increases and the going gets harder."

Others in the field tend to agree. One reason is simply that ageing is very complex and we do not know enough to make sensible predictions. Caleb Finch of the University of Southern California says: "I have a simple view: we don't know what we don't know about ageing processes. So, what can be said on future longevity?"

Linda Partridge of University College London's Centre for Research on Ageing, well known for work on fruit flies, backs Professor Kirkwood. In any case, she adds, "I think that we should be working to promote health during ageing rather than increases in lifespan per se." Either way, she believes that "progress will be gradual and based on existing promising areas of work, rather than saltatory and based on unproven approaches".

Her colleague David Gems, who works on nematode worms, is optimistic that the basic biology of ageing will be understood in the next decade or two. But he stresses that how easily this translates into treating or preventing ageing-related diseases depends on what ageing really turns out to be: "There's a huge margin of uncertainty." He suggests that cancer treatments are a better historical guide than, say, antibiotics - and most cancers remain incurable.

Martin Brand of the Medical Research Council's Dunn Human Nutrition Unit in Cambridge also urges caution. "There have been spectacular increases in lifespan caused by simple treatments and mutations in model organisms," he concedes. But he is mindful that flies and mice in the laboratory tend to live shorter lives than wild strains. "I worry that these results can be explained as putting right bad husbandry of the model organisms rather than affecting ageing itself."

Questions 1– 6

Look at the following people and the list of statements below.

Match each statement with the correct person.

You may use any answer more than once.

	1.	The condition of the body starts to decline when we can't have offspring.
	2.	Only two things are predictable in life.
	3.	Living longer is less important than how healthy we are as we age.
	4.	Restricted diets seem to result in a longer life for mice.
	5.	People make ridiculous statements about how long we can live.
	6.	We can't predict the future because we don't know enough about the ageing process.

List of People	
A	Aubrey de Grey
B	Caleb Finch
C	David Gems
D	Linda Partridge
E	Benjamin Franklin
F	Martin Brand
G	Tom Kirkwood
H	Author

Reading – Yes / No / Not Given

> **IELTS Tips**
>
> You MUST write – YES, NO, NOT GIVEN – on your answer sheet.
>
> Answers are usually in order.

One of the most important things to remember when answering a Yes/No/Not Given question is that everything in the text is always correct. What you have to do is decide whether or not the question sentence is also correct. The instructions given to you in the test state that you must write:

YES	*if the statement agrees with the writer's claims*
NO	*if the statement contradicts the writer's claims*
NOT GIVEN	*if it is impossible to say what the writer thinks about this*

Answering the YES question is usually not so difficult because the question sentence will match the information shown in the text. The order of information might be different and synonyms will probably have been used but, nevertheless, the information is the same.

However, many students get confused between NO and NOT GIVEN and cannot always decide between the two. If the question sentence contradicts information in the text, for example, if it states that, *he has to arrive at his office before 9 o'clock everyday* but the text says that, *he always gets to his office at 9.30* then clearly both pieces of information cannot be true and so the answer is NO.

If you are sure that the question sentence is not the same as information in the text then ask yourself this, "Is there no, or not enough, evidence to prove that the question statement contradicts the information in the text?" You might read, for instance, that, *the man always gets to the office on time* but doesn't say what time. In this case, you know that the answer must be NOT GIVEN because it neither matches the information in the text nor contradicts it.

When writing the answers in the answer sheet it is very important to do this correctly. Remember: you must write the answers in full – YES, NO, NOT GIVEN – you might have points deducted if you write – Y, N, NG – and certainly TRUE, FALSE or T, F would be seen as wrong. If you have run out of time and have to guess, pick one answer, for instance NO, and write this as an answer for ALL of the questions; you can guarantee that some of them will be correct.

British Eccentric

Every once in a while, says New York magazine, there appears a character who floats above "the wretched, amoral, meatheads" of Wall Street. Andrew J Hall is such a man.

The UK-born commodities trader, who heads a "secretive unit" at Citigroup known as Phibro (so secretive there are no publicly available pictures of him), has made a personal $250m killing from oil futures as well as generating 10% of the bank's total net income last year.

Yet he maintains a wonderfully eccentric lifestyle. Not only is he one of the world's most obsessive art collectors, but he regularly leaves the office early either to row "or to practice calisthenics with a ballet teacher".

"Trading" may be the wrong word to describe what Hall, 57, does best, says Portfolio.com: he makes very large, long-term bets, and sits back. The genesis of his latest punt came in 2003 when he anticipated "an important shift in the way the world valued oil", says the Wall Street Journal. Prices had ranged from $10 to $30 a barrel for more than a decade, with the trend so pronounced that contracts on future prices were some 20% cheaper than the "spot", or current, price.

Hall was convinced that growth in demand, from China and India was starting to outstrip supply and that "long-term and short-term energy prices would soon abandon" this relationship. He "bet big", buying up every long-term contract going. By 2005 he had made a fortune. Citigroup is lucky to have him.

Yet Andy Hall has been operating in relative obscurity for years. Most of his recent press coverage homes in on his career as an art collector, notably on the controversial installation (and subsequent forced removal) of a massive, 80-foot long concrete artwork in the back garden of his Connecticut mansion, which one neighbour compared to "a bad chunk of Interstate 95".

A naturalised US citizen, Hall is married to Christine, "a slim, fashionable and slightly giddy Englishwoman" who shares his passion for art and advises on purchases, notes the New Yorker. Details of Hall's early career are sketchy. An Oxford chemistry graduate, he started at BP before joining Phibro, then owned by Salomon Brothers, in 1982. It went well. By 1991, he boasted a $23m pay packet and a seat on the board and had made Phibro much more than just a trading outfit: it also had sizeable physical assets, including four oil refineries, and Hall harboured ambitions to build it into an "oil well to petrol pump" operation to rival the leading majors. Those plans were scuppered when he was wrong-footed during the first Gulf War, losing some $100m when the oil price plunged.

A weakened Salomon Brothers was eventually sold to Travelers Group in 1997, becoming part of Citigroup a year later. Since then, Citigroup's "stepchild" has thrived on a policy of "benign neglect", says the Wall Street Journal. Run in a former dairy farm in Westport, Connecticut, Phibro has been scaled back to "a skeletal crew" and keeps 20%–30% of its trading gains.

Citi's new chief, Vikram Pandit, is reportedly keen to rein in this "under-leveraged brand" and fold it into Citi's asset management arm – an idea Hall has dismissed as "a complete non-starter". More fool Pandit if he persists, says Portfolio.com. "Has he never heard of what happened to the goose that laid the golden eggs?" If push comes to shove, Hall may well break out on his own.

Hall doesn't just confine his bets to oil and gas, says The Wall Street Journal. In the late 1990s, he was big on silver (numbering Warren Buffett's Berkshire Hathaway among his clients) and has been were .

active in unusual commodities, too. "Twice in the past decade he has assembled big stockpiles of rhodium [used in catalytic converters]. He got out both times at around ten times his money." His secret, says a fellow oil man, is an ability to block out noise. When Hall "locks in on an idea, he'll take it to the extreme".

The same is true of his $100m art collection. "As with oil, he sometimes zeroes in on out-of-favour artists, often snapping up entire shows." Hall loves taking bets on contemporary US work, but his current obsession is for German neo-expressionists, such as Georg Baselitz. He so rates the latter that he not only has many of Baselitz's canvasses, but has also acquired his 1,000-year-old German castle to keep them in.

Hall approaches art collecting "with the fanatical dedication of an oarsman", says the New Yorker. But he hates galleries. "I hate shopping, I hate salespeople, and I had this feeling that gallerists were salespeople. There's a whole in-ness, with regard to which galleries are hot; that I can't stand."

The chief beneficiary of his largesse is enfant terrible of the New York art world, Leo Koenig – a German-born dealer with connections to some of Hall's favourite artists. Much of the collection is housed in a New York storage facility. When Hall visits, he seems to lose himself. "Wow, we have great stuff," he is said to murmur.

Questions 1– 8

Do the following statements agree with the claims of the writer in?

In boxes 1– 8 on your answer sheet, write

YES	*if the statement agrees with the writer's claims*
NO	*if the statement contradicts the writer's claims*
NOT GIVEN	*if it is impossible to say what the writer thinks about this*

1. Andrew J Hall is an amoral meathead.
2. Hall frequently leaves the office to argue with people. *NO*
3. China and India are the world's main oil consumers. *YES*
4. Hall's wife helps make financial decisions. *YES*
5. Phibro had to sell its oil refineries because of the Gulf War.
6. Travellers Group became part of Citigroup in 1998. *YES*
7. Georg Baselitz is Hall's favourite artist. *YES*
8. Hall hates galleries because they are too hot. *YES*

Reading – Matching Headlines

In this kind of matching exercise there are three or four more headings than you need. Skim the passage quickly to get an overview of the main idea for each paragraph. Underline keywords. Next look at the list of headings and match those that you can without rereading the passage. Remember to cross out the headings you have used. Finally, read the paragraphs that you have not matched more carefully then choose (or guess) the best headings.

Almas: The Mongolian Man-Beast

Questions 1– 6

The reading passage has six paragraphs A– F.

Choose the correct heading for each paragraph from the list of headings below.

List of Headings

i	Lamaism	vi	Living in Mongolia
ii	First account of almases	vii	Relic hominid theory
iii	Missing link	viii	Funding expeditions
iv	Monasteries and medicine	ix	New discoveries
v	Borrowed tales from Tibet?	x	Mysterious mountain men

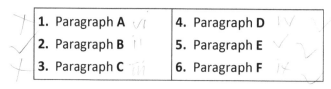

1. Paragraph **A**   vi
2. Paragraph **B**   ii
3. Paragraph **C**   iii
4. Paragraph **D**   iv
5. Paragraph **E**   v
6. Paragraph **F**   ix

A   Mongolia usually evokes images of nomadic herdsmen riding across vast grasslands but along the western border with Russia the Altai Mountains stretch for over a thousand kilometres, their permanently ice-capped peaks rising above 4000 metres. From these mountains have long come reports of a mysterious human-like creature called an almas. Sightings have become increasingly rare over the past hundred years, but according to old accounts, almas are described as being similar in height to that of modern Mongolians, hairy, having massive jaws, receding chins and prominent eyebrow ridges. They are thought to be mainly nocturnal, are unaggressive and usually avoid contact with humans.

B   The earliest description of an almas appears in the memoirs of a Bavarian nobleman, Hans Schiltberger, who was taken prisoner by the Turks in the early 1400s and sent eastward to serve a Mongol prince. "In the mountains themselves live wild people, who have nothing in common with other human beings. A pelt covers the entire body of these creatures. Only the hands and face are free of hair."

Giving his seemingly incredible account some credibility is the fact that he also mentions the Przewalski horse (*Equus ferus przewalskii*), the last remaining wild species of horse which was unknown in Europe until centuries later.

C   A few scientists such as Myra Shackley, however, have suggested that the almas is (or at least "was") a real creature, and that it could be a remnant population of hominids, either *homo erectus* or Neanderthals. Neanderthals – mankind's closest cousins – lived in Central Asia, the Middle East and Europe, and are thought to have died out 25,000-30,000 years ago. Most scientists dismiss the almas as mere folklore because no physical evidence has been found. Over the decades there has been the occasional "find" (hair, a skull, droppings) but tests have shown them to be either of human origin or from known animals.

D   Many accounts of almases seem to be tied up with Mongolia's pre-communist Buddhism. In 1837 a pilgrim called Luvsandonoi (Mongolians typically use just a single name) found the body of a dead male almas in the Gobi Desert. He reportedly gave the skin, head, and limbs to the Galbyn Ulaan Sahiur monastery. Lamas stuffed the skin. The stuffed almas was said to be hairy but with some human-like features. There are various other descriptions of monasteries with almas artefacts – even one with a complete stuffed almas. Unfortunately, communist purges in the 1930s led to the destruction of all but one of the countries more than 500 monasteries, and these artefacts were destroyed or disappeared. An interesting reoccurring element of almas stories is the use of the bile (a digestive juice produced by the liver) from the gall bladder as a medicine. It was highly prized and used by lama doctors to treat a variety of disorders. Interestingly, bile from the gall bladder of black bears has long been used in traditional Chinese medicine.

E   One possible explanation for the almas is that it is folklore imported alongside Tibetan Buddhism from the Himalayas. From medieval times until the early twentieth century, Buddhism dominated religious, cultural and educational life in Mongolia. There were important ties with Tibet and it was not uncommon for the religious leaders and devout followers to make the pilgrimage to the holy city of Lhasa where they would have heard the tales of the yetis, and seen various supposed yeti artefacts in monasteries. Currently, the weight of scientific opinion is that the yeti is a mythical creature born of a combination of bear sightings and folklore.

F   Two recent scientific bombshells give the remnant hominid theory a boost. First, the discovery of a new human species *Homo floresiensis* (nicknamed the Hobbit) and the startling fact that it occupied the Indonesian island of Flores until perhaps as recently as 12,000 years ago. Even more relevant to the almas mystery is the 2008 discovery of a female finger bone in a cave in the Siberian section of the Altai Mountains. An international team of scientists from the Max Planck Institute for Evolutionary Anthropology in Leipzig, Germany have worked on the mitochondrial DNA from the finger bone. They announced in 2010 that it was from a previously unknown hominid species that lived in the Altai Mountains about 35,000 years ago.

Summary Completion

Questions 7–10

Complete the summary using the list of words, A– P, below.

A hairy human-like creature with **7.** ....*G*..... facial features called an almas has, for centuries, been reported in the Altai Mountains of western Mongolia, though sightings are now very rare. The earliest European **8.** ....*J*........ to almases dates from the 1400s. According to one theory, the almas could be a remnant population of hominids, either *homo erectus* or Neanderthals. As no physical evidence has been found, most scientists believe the almas to be a **9.** ....*D*........ creature. Buddhist monasteries are said to have had almas body parts but these disappeared during purges in the 1930s. The origin of almas stories may lie in Mongolian pilgrims borrowing **10.** ....*L*....... of the yeti and artefacts from Tibet. Mitochondrial DNA from a finger bone found in the Altai Mountains in 2008 suggests an unknown hominid species lived there about 35,000 years ago.

A	B	C	D	E	F	G	H
artefacts	journal	remnant	mythical	receding	traveller	primitive	modern
I	**J**	**K**	**L**	**M**	**N**	**O**	**P**
tales	reference	Buddhism	story	Himalayan	unknown	relic	mysteries

Writing Task 2 – **Brainstorming** – Developing Your Ideas

Before writing the introduction it is a good idea to begin to develop what will go into the main body. This helps you reconfirm that you understand the meaning of the Task 2 statement and may help when writing the introduction and in particular the 'topic importance'.

Exercise

Look at the Task 2 statement below and then try to decide which of the brainstorming suggestions are correct and which ones are incorrect. Give reasons why.

Task 2

In countries like Japan people often work beyond the traditional age of retirement. One reason for this is because people are living longer than ever before. This has made it much more difficult for university graduates to find a job. A solution often put forward for reducing unemployment is for the government to enforce a lower retirement age. To what extent do you agree.

Brainstorming Suggestions

- Develop reasons why people live longer.
- Offer ideas explaining why people in Japan work past retirement age.
- Explain why it is a good idea to retire earlier.
- Offer further solutions for reducing unemployment.
- Give the advantages and disadvantages of retiring early.
- State whether or not you agree with the Task 2 opinion.

Exercise

Now, spend 5 minutes developing as many ideas for this Task 2 statement as you can. Which ideas do you think are more important? Decide what your topic direction will be and then write your introduction.

Exercise

Now do the same with this Task 2 question. Brainstorm for ideas and then write the introduction.

Task 2

What are the pros and cons of city life when compared with life in a more rural setting?

Writing Task 2 – **Brainstorming** – Developing Your Ideas

Ideas that you develop while brainstorming can come from things you have experienced, read in a newspaper or on the Internet, seen on TV, heard on the radio or talked about with friends. Any of these ideas can be used in Task 2 writing. These are the supporting points to your topic.

Using only two paragraphs in the middle is possible but means that you have to develop each idea more than when using three paragraphs. If these ideas are well developed and help to support and strengthen your topic direction, you have a much better chance of obtaining a good IELTS grade.

Exercise
Before writing down any ideas, read the Task 2 statement below and then write down the topic, topic importance and then write a topic direction sentence.

Task 2
A rapidly increasing global population will lead to many social and environmental problems unless something is done to address this impending catastrophe. Suggest ways to help slow down this trend.

Exercise
Now look at the Task 2 problem/solution statement again and try to think of as many ideas as possible that might help this problem. How practical and how effective do you think they would be? Can you think of any countries where they have already tried some of these ideas? Have they been successful?

Exercise
Now look at an example for one of the middle three paragraphs for this Task 2 essay and then complete the paragraph below by adding the words from the box.

My first recommendation would be to provide **1.** _____ for parents who do not exceed the stated maximum number of **2.** _____. In addition, the **3.** _____ could also introduce sex education lessons into the **4.** _____ and establish **5.** _____ clinics in the more rural areas of the country. Finally, the introduction of a **6.** _____ that would ease the **7.** _____ of the poorer families would also help.

A children	B family planning	C financial burden	D government
E national curriculum	F tax incentives	G welfare system	

Exercise
Do you think that the paragraph you have completed is suitable for an IELTS Task 2 essay?

Writing Task 2 – **Writing the Essay** – Introductions

An introduction should be about fifty words in length. Less than this and you might have failed to write an introduction that does what it should do. More than fifty words and you might have started to write too much information and might be moving on to develop the main ideas of the essay. The introduction is not the place to do this.

A simple introduction could be, "This is an essay about the deforestation of tropical rainforests and the link to global warming." This does tell you what the essay is about but it would not impress the examiner.

Introducing the Topic

To write a more effective introduction you need to appreciate more clearly why you are writing it. One answer could be, "I am writing it because it is in my IELTS test." This isn't a wrong answer but thinking this way is not the best way to focus your mind on the task ahead. It would be better to say, "This is an interesting topic and I want the opportunity to express my views." If you don't find it an interesting topic, then think of the people who would. For instance, a topic on education would be of interest to educationalists, teachers, the Department of Education, students, and parents.

Exercise

Look at the following topics and write down the people or groups of people that would want to read an essay about these topics. This information could be used to develop the topic of the essay. Several examples are given for you.

	Topic	Interested People / Groups
1.	endangered animals	zoologists
2.	higher divorce rates	social workers
3.	environmental problems	environmentalists
4.	sex education	health officials
5.	health issues	doctors

Topic Importance (or Thesis Statement)

After deciding who would be interested in this topic, you can then think about the reasons why this topic is important. For instance, a topic based on the opinion, "Should stronger gun laws be introduced?" is an important issue to discuss due to the continued use of guns in crime-related violence and the increasing number of guns in society. Very often the topic and topic importance can be written in one sentence.

Topic Direction

Now that you have written the topic and topic importance, it is now time to state the direction of the essay. What is the purpose of the essay? What do you hope to achieve? This can be seen as your response to the instructions given to you.

Writing Task 2 – Developing a Writing Style

To have a better chance of getting a good grade in the writing test, it is important to develop a writing style that is formal but at the same time shows signs of the academic style needed when you go to study at university.

Exercise

With a partner try to think of what would make a better writing style to the one you use now. What do you think the examiner will look for when he is reading your essay? Look at one of your essays and try to imagine what the examiner would say. Write your ideas in the space provided below.

....

....

....

....

....

Exercise

Now use the list of factors you have listed above to help you alter the paragraph below. Do you like the style of writing? Why or why not? DO NOT add any further information to the article. The challenge is to try and improve this by only using the writing skills you have discussed.

Remember: ideas, opinions, examples and the development of these are essential but the way you present all of this information makes up a big percentage – about 25% – of your final grade.

> Nowadays, most people travel by air if they have to travel a long distance. This was not always so. If people had to go on a long overseas trip 100 years ago they went by boat. The trip took a long time and was often really rough and uncomfortable. First class passengers were far more comfortable than second class passengers. Second class passengers could not go into first class areas. Many people preferred to travel on a ship, which only had one class. Seventy years ago many people travelled by sea. Air travel has only become popular since the 1960s. This is because it's cheaper, safe, convenient & quick.

Exercise

When analyzing your own writing, did you think about:

1. joining sentences together to make some sentences longer
2. using synonyms and other techniques to reduce repeated vocabulary
3. replacing informal/simple vocabulary with higher level vocabulary
4. putting information into a more logical order
5. using cohesive phrases
6. removing any problems mentioned in the informal/formal writing list on page 50.
7. correcting grammar
8. correcting spelling
9. using paragraphs
10. is your handwriting legible?

Task 2 – **Writing Style** – Using more Academic Vocabulary

Another important aspect of writing in a more academic style is determined by which words are used to express your ideas. Higher level vocabulary is clearly better but how do you begin to decide which words to use and which words to change?

Exercise
Look at the following sentences and decide which of the two sentences (**A** or **B**) are more academic and write your answer in the box. Check your answers with your partner and try to decide what makes certain sentences more academic.

			A or B
1.	A	He carried out research to prove his theory.	
	B	He conducted research to prove his theory.	
2.	A	He invested a lot of money in the project.	
	B	He put up a lot of money for the project.	
3.	A	The company asked for compensation for the delay in dealing with their order.	
	B	The company requested compensation for the delay in processing their order.	
4.	A	University tuition fees went up by over 60% last year.	
	B	University tuition fees increased by over 60% last year.	
5.	A	The local factories give off a lot of toxic fumes.	
	B	The local factories emit a lot of toxic fumes.	

Informal writing tends to use more multi-word verbs. These are often referred to as phrasal verbs and can be defined as a combination of a verb and preposition, a verb and an adverb, or a verb with both an adverb and a preposition. Examples from the exercise above are - carried out, put up, asked for, dealing with, went up, give off. By turning these multi-word verbs into single verbs you have increased both the level of formality and the academic style of your sentence.

Exercise
Make the sentences below more academic by replacing the multi-word verbs in italics with one of the single verbs in the box.

Note: you might have to change the form of the verb.

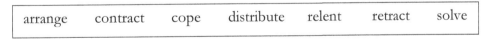

| arrange | contract | cope | distribute | relent | retract | solve |

1. After threatening to hit me, the man *backed down* and apologized.

2. Eventually, the newspaper *took back* its accusations.

3. Many people *came down with* pneumonia in the severe winter of 1905.

4. Only the professor in the Math Department was able to *figure out* the problem.

5. He used to work in a soup kitchen *passing out* hot meals to the homeless.

6. Despite earning a very low salary he was able to *get by*.

7. He *set up* a meeting for the following weekend.

Writing Task 2 – **Writing the Essay** – Agree and Disagree

Task 2.
Single-sex schools are better than coeducational schools. Discuss both views.

Step 1 .... Read the Task 2 instructions carefully

Step 2 .... Decide which type of essay it is – Type **A**, **B**, or **C**   (see page 48)

Step 3 .... Understand the topic

Step 4 .... Select your topic importance

> **a.** background information
> **b.** what people / groups are interested?
> **c.** what is changing in society?

You will find that the importance of most Task 2 essays focuses on something changing in society. This might be a change for the better or for the worse but it is always a change that creates an interest in or concern about something. So always ask yourself, "What is changing in society that has made this topic important?" In this particular example, the topic is important because, as competition increases to get the best education schools can offer, it is important to decide which type of education is better.

Step 5 .... Select your topic direction (agree or disagree)

Step 6 .... Main Body; use one or more of the brainstorming techniques shown on page 53 and list points on both sides of the argument

Agree	Disagree

Exercise
Now write your essay using four paragraphs.

Remember: You must include opinions for 'agree' and 'disagree' in order to make your essay balanced. It also shows the examiner that you have considered both sides of the argument – an important skill in more academic styles of writing. If your topic direction is 'agree' then paragraph two should discuss the opposite point of view, paragraphs three and four should be your opinion. The reverse is true if you disagree.

Reading – Summary and Multiple-Choice

Mr. Ben Ahore, Central Bank of Nigeria

Lagos, Nigeria

Tel: 234-1-555 6873

March 13, 2011

Dear Mr. Smith,

I have been requested by the Nigerian National Petroleum Company to contact you for assistance in resolving a matter. The Nigerian National Petroleum Company has recently concluded a large number of contracts for oil exploration in the sub-Sahara region. The contracts have immediately produced money equalling US$40,000,000. The Nigerian National Petroleum Company is desirous of oil exploration in other parts of the world. However, because of certain regulations of the Nigerian Government, it is unable to move these funds to another region.

Your assistance is requested as a non-Nigerian citizen to assist the Nigerian National Petroleum Company, and also the Central Bank of Nigeria, in moving these funds out of Nigeria. If the funds can be transferred to your name, in your United States account, then you can forward the funds as directed by the Nigerian National Petroleum Company. In exchange for your accommodating services, the Nigerian National Petroleum Company would agree to allow you to retain US$4 million of this amount.

However, to be a legitimate transferee of this money according to Nigerian law, you must presently be a depositor of at least US$100,000 in a Nigerian bank which is regulated by the Central Bank of Nigeria.

If it is possible for you to assist us, we would be most grateful. It is best that you meet with us in person in Lagos, and that during your visit I introduce you to the representatives of the Nigerian National Petroleum Company, as well as with certain officials of the Central Bank of Nigeria.

Please call me at your earliest convenience on 234-1-555-6873. Time is of the essence in this matter; very quickly the Nigerian Government will realize that the Central Bank is maintaining this amount on deposit, and attempt to tax the funds.

Yours truly,

Ben Ahore

Adapted from a passage from: *www.quatloos.com*

Unit 12

Questions 1–8

Complete the summary below.

Choose NO MORE THAN THREE WORDS AND/OR A NUMBER from the passage for each answer.

The Nigerian National Petroleum Company (NNPC) requires your help moving forty million dollars earned from oil exploration contracts out of the country. Because of government 1. _Certain regulations_, the assistance of a non-Nigerian citizen is needed to do this. In return for allowing these funds to be transferred through your account, NNPC will pay you 2. _US$4 million_. However, to legally 3. _transfer_ the money, you must have a minimum of 4. _US$100,000_ in a bank account in a government-approved Nigerian bank. If possible, please come to 5. _Lagos_ where you will be introduced to 6. _rep. of NNPC_ from the company and officials from the 7. _Central bank of Nigeria_. Call 234-1-555-6873 ASAP to arrange things before the government tries to 8. _take_ the money.

Questions 9–10

Choose the appropriate letter A–D.

9. The Nigerian National Petroleum Company says it wants to use the US$40 million

   A for personal reasons.
   B to look for oil in other countries. ✓
   C for government regulations.
   D in order to establish an overseas bank account.

10. Although the writer is offering a large amount of money, the problem is that before getting the money it is necessary to

   A go to Nigeria.
   B break the law.
   C put US$100,000 in a Nigerian bank account. ✓
   D form a company.

Note: Multiple Choice reading questions often end with one that tests overall understanding of the text, the general point of the article, or the purpose/point of view of the writer. Unlike other questions that relate to specific parts of the text, these ones require you to use your common sense.

Reading – Sentence Completion

Vancouver

Vancouver is quite different from virtually any other city in North America. Despite the fact it is a large modern cosmopolitan city, it seems to have a relaxed small-town, close-to-nature feel about it. There is little comparison with other large Canadian cities such as Toronto or Montreal, which are more akin to the large eastern US centres like New York and Chicago. Vancouver, like all large North American cities, is a conglomerate of high-rise cubic office towers, although urban planners have kept the heights down. There are, however, some notable exceptions such as the Marine Building at the north foot of Burrard Street, once the tallest structure in the British Empire, the courthouse at Howe & Robson, and the library at Georgia & Hamilton.

Vancouver offers a wide range of attractions catering to all tastes but those with only a day to spare cannot be better advised than to take one of the many organized excursions recommended by the Vancouver Tourist Office.

Stanley Park, a 1,000-acre nature preserve, is Vancouver's best-known landmark and a must for any visitor. It was established in 1887 and, in the opinion of many, is the most beautiful urban park in the world. Contrary to popular belief, this park was not established through the foresight of the city council of the day, but at the urging of a real estate developer called Oppenheimer. He is now considered the father of Stanley Park. All areas of the park are accessible to the public except for Dead Man's Island, which has a small naval base.

The EcoWalk is a fun and informative way to see the park. The guide gives information on the trees, plants, birds and animals as well as on the rich aboriginal culture and legends of the park. The walking is medium paced, taking 3 hours to complete and covering 5 miles of relatively flat paved and graveled trails over selected seawall and forest paths. This walk is suitable for families, including active seniors.

There is also a world class aquarium in the park and was the first to have killer whales in captivity and probably the first one to stop making them into a side-show. The aquarium feels the purpose in keeping the whales, namely re-educating the public and stopping the hunting of them, has been accomplished. In 2000, the last remaining killer whale at the aquarium was sold to Sealand in California, where it died shortly after arriving. The main threat to the park is the sheer volume of people who want to be in it. Efforts are being made to restrict the amount of automobile traffic passing through it. One of the ultimate goals is to eliminate the causeway leading to Lions Gate Bridge but this will not likely occur until well into the 21st century.

Beaches are also a big attraction and temperatures are usually high enough to tempt most people to have a swim. However, one of the biggest days on these beaches is on New Year's Day when the annual "Polar Bear Swim" attracts several hundred die-hard individuals out to prove that Vancouver is a year round swimming destination.

Chinatown is North America's third largest, in terms of area, after San Francisco and New York. It is steeped in history and is well worth walking around. It is most active on Sundays when people head to any of a wide selection of restaurants that offer dim sum. Chinatown also contains the world's thinnest building at only 1.8 metres wide.

Unit 12

Questions 1– 7

Do the following questions agree with the information given in the passage? Write:

Yes	*if the statement agrees with the information*
No	*if the statement contradicts the statement information*
Not Given	*if there is no information on this in the passage*

1. When compared with Toronto, Vancouver is very similar. *No* ✓

2. If time is limited, it is inadvisable to go on any of the official day trips available. *yes* ✗

3. Oppenheimer built Stanley Park with the help of the city council. *No* ✗

4. The majority of the park is open to the public. *Yes* ✓

5. The Toronto aquarium killed its last killer whale. *No* ✓

6. The main problem in the park is that the people are too loud. *Not given* ✓

7. Vancouver's Chinatown has the third largest Chinese population in North America. *No* ✓

Questions 8– 12

*Using **NO MORE THAN THREE WORDS** taken from the reading passage, answer the following questions.*

8.   What famous building was once the highest in the British Empire? *Marine building* ✓

9.   What was the profession of the park's founding father? *Real state Developer* ✓

10. What is one of the final aims in the park? *Eliminate the causeway* ✓

11. What event tries to encourage people to swim? *Polar Bear Swim* ✓

12. What can you eat in Chinatown? *dim sum* ✓

Questions 13– 15

*Complete each of the following sentences with **NO MORE THAN THREE WORDS**.*

13. Interesting facts about the indigenous population of Canada are provided on the ___*Hardy bark*___ ✗

14. It is possible to finish the EcoWalk with a medium- ___*paced*___ gait in 3 hours. ✓

15. The aquarium's objective has been achieved because they have ___*re-educated*___ the public.

Writing Task 2 – **Writing the essay** – Problems and solutions

Task 2

Stress is now becoming a major problem in many cities around the world. Give some suggestions to control this trend.

Step 1 .... Read the Task 2 instructions carefully

Step 2 .... Decide which type of essay it is – Type **A**, **B**, or **C**   (see page 48)

Step 3 .... Understand the topic

Step 4 .... Select your topic importance

> **a.** background information
> **b.** what people/groups are interested?
> **c.** what is changing in society?

The topic importance in a problem/solution essay is based on showing that the cause (or problem) is creating an effect on society in some way. In the example, the cause of stress could be resulting in physical and psychological health problems, higher divorce rates, higher suicide rates, lowered work efficiency and so on. If the cause of stress did not result in any effect, it would be difficult to explain why the topic is important so think carefully about this before writing your essay.

Step 5 .... Select your topic direction (there is only one – solve the problem)

Step 6 .... Main Body; use one or more of the brainstorming techniques shown on page 53 and list points on both sides of the argument

Cause - problem	Effect - topic importance	Solution - for the cause/problem
	physical and psychological problems	
	higher divorce rates	
	higher suicide rates	
	lowered work efficiency	

Exercise

Now write your essay using a four-paragraph essay.

Remember: you can include causes of the problem in paragraph two and solutions to the stated causes in paragraphs three and four. A sample essay is provided in the answer section of the book.

Writing Task 2 – **Main Body** – Coherence

Coherence is the term used to express the smooth flow of information within one sentence, from one sentence to the next, and from one paragraph to another. The simple reason for wanting to write coherently is that your essay will be easier to understand. It will also help you to get a higher grade in the IELTS test.

There are a number of different ways to create coherence but perhaps the easiest way, although many students still do this incorrectly, is by using transitional phrases. These act as signposts that highlight the connection between what you have just read and what follows. When you read the phrase, "For instance", it is clear that an example of a previously stated point is going to be given. The word, "However", tells you that a contrast to the previous information is now going to be presented.

Understanding, and being able to effectively use a wide range of these transitional phrases is essential. Use these words and phrases to highlight your logic and allow the reader - the IELTS examiner, your professor - to understand your essays more easily.

Addition	also, and, equally important, in addition, furthermore, moreover, on top of that
Cause and Effect	as a result, because, consequently, for, hence, owing to the fact that, since, so that, thereby, therefore, thus
Comparison	also, in the same way, likewise, similarly
Conclusion	all in all, altogether, finally, in brief, in conclusion, in essence, in short, in summary, on the whole, to conclude, to summarise, to sum up
Contrast	although, and yet, but, but at the same time, conversely, despite that, even so, even though, however, in contrast, in spite of, instead, nevertheless, on the other hand, whereas, while, yet
Emphasis	above all, a central issue, a key factor, indeed, in fact, it should be noted that, most important of all, most noteworthy, most significant, the main point is that, the principal issue, undoubtedly, without doubt, without exception
Example	for example, for instance, indeed, in fact, in particular, namely, that is, to illustrate
Restating	in other words, put another way, that is to say, in other words
Time Order	after a while, afterward, again, and then, before, earlier, finally, in the first place, in the past, last, lately, meanwhile, next, now, presently, secondly, shortly, simultaneously, soon, still, subsequently, then, thereafter, until, until now, when

Besides

The word 'besides' is often used by students as an alternative to 'in addition' but is more often used in spoken English rather than written as it is too informal for this style of writing.

Writing Task 2 – **Coherence** – Transitional Phrases

Although transitional phrases are very important, we should not overuse them. In IELTS, there is a tendency for students to use them too often. A typical, but acceptable, style for IELTS is shown in the extract below about recycling computers (e-waste).

Exercise
Complete each sentence by adding the correct transitional phrase from the box.

E-waste

1. ………..……. in e-waste disposal is that many computer parts contain toxic material **2.** ……….……. lead and mercury. **3.** ……….......……, due to a poorly-developed collection system, levels of dumping of personal computers and laptops are increasing at over three times that of other solid waste. **4.** ………....……, toxins enter the soil and from here they may run into streams and rivers and **5.** ……….....…… enter the human food chain. Mercury, **6.** ……….....……, can cause a range of health problems including headaches, tremors and learning difficulties. Consequently, a new bill is about to be passed that offers incentives to both companies and individuals to recycle their e-waste.

7. ……….....…… of recycling e-waste is that metals like tin, silicon, copper, and even gold can be recycled and used again in the production of other products. **8.** ……….…..……, continued efforts to increase e-waste recycling will help reduce the need for costly and environmentally damaging extraction of these metals from mines.

a central issue	an additional benefit	as a result
for instance however	indeed subsequently	such as

The ability to write coherently, however, is not achieved simply by filling your essay full of transitional phrases. A coherent flow of information is developed by using a number of different methods that help create a good writing style. So, rather like a paper trail that links clues at a murder scene to the murderer, these techniques will link the writer's ideas from beginning to end. The better the trail, the better the comprehension of the text.

Exercise
Look at the paragraph below and rearrange the sentences so that each sentence is in a more logical position.

Remember: This paragraph is now in a less than logical order but because each sentence makes sense, many students will say that it is a good paragraph. Always think of the flow of information. This creates the logic.

A Gap Year

This year offers them the chance to experience new things as well as time to reflect on their future career. For instance, they can travel, work for a charity, or study non-academic skills during what is known as a gap year. However, students are now realizing that education does not always have to come from the classroom. A career that, perhaps, will change because of the time they spend experiencing the real world. Formal education is seen by many people as the only way to become a well educated person.

Task 2 – Expressing Personal Opinions

Another important part of writing a successful Task 2 assignment is the way you state your opinion. You must sound confident that your opinion is correct. If you introduce your ideas by saying; *it might* be *a good idea to*, or *it seems to be better than the other*, you will leave the reader with the feeling that you are not sure that your opinions are right.

An easy way to present your opinions is by using expressions like: *I feel, I think, In my opinion* and so on. However, as you begin to develop a better writing style, try to use slightly more complex and more interesting phrases. The style you use to do this will become a part of how you express yourself not only in writing but when talking in a more formal setting.

Agreeing, Disagreeing

I am completely convinced that _____ is better than _____

There is no doubt in my mind that _____

Some people suggest that _____ is better than _____

Problems, Solutions

I would recommend that the government _____

As far as I am concerned, the best course of action would be to _____

It is essential that the government imposes stronger laws in order to _____

A complete ban on _____ is the only possible solution to this problem.

Task 2 – **Transitional Phrases** – Coherence

A piece of writing that has no real structure is really not much more than just a list of ideas and examples. Perhaps your ideas and examples offer good supporting points to your topic direction but without the necessary linking transitional words and phrases, the connections between each piece of information will be missing. The end result is an article that isn't easy to read and, more importantly, you won't get the grade that you deserve.

Developing the skills needed to create a better feeling of continuity – and in particular a smooth flow of ideas in the three middle paragraphs – can be achieved quite quickly if you learn which words and phrases should be used in each particular situation.

Exercise
Look again at the Task 2 statement shown on page 63.

In countries like Japan people often work beyond the traditional age of retirement. One reason for this is because people are living longer than ever before. This has made it much more difficult for university graduates to find a job. A solution often put forward for reducing unemployment is for the government to enforce a lower retirement age. Discuss.

Exercise
The paragraph below contains all the information from the three middle paragraphs of this essay. However, the sentences are in the wrong order. Try to separate this information into the three supporting paragraphs. Make sure that the flow of ideas fits the topic direction of disagreeing with the Task 2 statement.

While these opinions seem convincing, they fail to take into consideration that older people have more experience not only within their area of expertise but also in society as a whole. We only need to look at some of our world leaders, both past and present, to see that age has no bearing on the ability to do well in their job. Furthermore, the fact that they are young would allow them to be trained more easily and accept innovation and new technology in a way that older people could not. Indeed, university graduates would find it very difficult to relate to the different kinds of relationships that exist in the business world. Lastly, the attitude that older workers cannot change their vision or attitude because they are set in their ways is based on wishful thinking. Many people support the idea of reducing the age of retirement because this is seen as a way to give younger people more opportunities to get a job.

Writing Task 2 – **Sample Essay** – Coherence

Exercise
Try to put the words and phrases below in the correct place in the Task 2 essay.

I am going to discuss this topic	In conclusion, I firmly believe that
However	In my opinion, however, I firmly believe that
therefore	A good example of
Another point of concern is that	They feel that
Many people would agree that	As a consequence,

Task 2
An eternal problem that governments face is the need to ensure the safety of their citizens. One way to do this is to introduce stronger gun laws. Discuss both sides of this argument and give your opinion.

1. .... cities are becoming more and more violent and guns are too easy to buy. News items regularly report robberies or murders where guns were involved. 2. .... people are now afraid to leave their homes at night or travel in taxis on their own. 3. .... from both points of view and then conclude by giving my own opinion.

4. .... some people still feel that the introduction of stronger gun laws will have no effect on the increase in crime rate in cities. 5. .... any increase in gun usage is the result of a poor economy rather than inadequate gun laws. Any improvement will **6.** .... be the result of government intervention to rectify the economy rather than amendments to the existing gun laws.

7. .... gun laws should be much tougher than they are now. 8. .... a country that has shown that stricter gun laws do work is in the UK. The policemen walk the streets without guns and gun related crime is much lower than in the USA where it seems anyone can by a gun if they have the money. Other countries like Singapore have had similar results.

9. .... the number of homicides committed by children both at home and in school is increasing. Although the reasons for this social phenomenon are complex, the very least we can do is protect our children by introducing stronger gun laws. The people who own guns must be made more responsible for how and where they keep their firearms.

10. .... the best way to make the streets safer is by introducing new government legislation to make it more difficult to buy guns. Let us follow the example of countries where such measures have already been adopted and the results clearly seen.

Writing Task 2 – **Critical Analysis** – Coherence

You might write something and be very pleased with the result and look at it with great pride - a great piece of writing. Think again.

Did you take time to review what you wrote and try to look at it as a stranger would when reading it for the first time? It is very easy to become too attached to your writing but so difficult to delete part of your article when it took so long to write. To be a good writer you must be able to critically analyse your own work and be able to look beyond the hard work and see the mistakes.

Exercise
Look at the text below on Ho Chi Minh City and look for problems with coherence.

Ho Chi Minh City

Ho Chi Minh City in Vietnam is a fascinating destination for travelers to Southeast Asia. It is located on the Mekong River. It was once an important trading center for the French in Southeast Asia. The influence of French culture can still be felt. Many people, especially the older generations, learned French in school and still can speak it very well. Some cafes serve French-style bread and pastries in Ho Chi Minh City. Expensive hotels and restaurants serve French food. Many of the buildings in the city are built in French style. The Vietnamese and the French fought. The French eventually left the country. There are museums and monuments documenting the country's long – and often bloody – history. If you are looking for a unique city to visit in Southeast Asia, Ho Chi Minh City is an attractive choice.

Now try to rewrite this again and try to eliminate as much repeated vocabulary as possible.

Did you notice the number of times certain words have been used? Too many times! Too many times! This unnecessary repetition of vocabulary is quite common. A topic on crime, for instance, might result in a 250-word essay having the word – **crime** – written over 10 times. Eliminating this repetition makes information flow more smoothly but how can it be done?

Synonyms are a very effective way of getting rid of some of the repeated words but the examiner does not want to see ten different ways of saying – **crime**. Certainly if you are able to think of so many synonyms for one word this is very impressive but it is even more impressive if you can develop the skills to get rid of the repeated word in different ways.

Exercise
What other ways can you think of to eliminate repeated vocabulary? Discuss these ideas with a classmate.

Remember: sometimes repeated vocabulary is simply the result of the unnecessary repetition of information.

Task 2 – **Critical Analysis** – Coherence

The text on Ho Chi Minh City highlighted the problem of repeated vocabulary. This is something that you should always look for when reviewing your work. If you have been a little too generous with certain words, then consider:

1. using a synonym:
> e.g. **rich** – wealthy

2. joining sentences together:
> e.g. The **rich** are very privileged. The **rich** are often spoilt.
> The **rich** are very privileged but spoilt.

Notice the correct use of the transitional word – **but**. The two pieces of information form a contrast and so you need to use **but** NOT **and**.

3. expressing the word as a definition:
> e.g. **rich** people should …. – people who have a lot of money should ….

4. using pronouns:
> e.g. Therefore, **rich** people should use some of their money to help the poor.
> Therefore, **they** should use some of their money to help the poor.

Exercise
Now analyse the two short article extracts that follow and try to rewrite them to create better coherence.

DNA Fingerprinting

DNA fingerprinting was developed by an English geneticist by the name of Alec Jeffreys in 1983. DNA fingerprinting is often used to help solve murder cases. DNA fingerprinting is able to indentify the linear sequence of four nucleotide bases; adenine, cytosine, guanine, and thymine present in genetic material and then match the sample to a person, living or dead. The process is very effective. DNA fingerprinting was first used in 1986 when a skeleton was discovered ten years after being wrapped in a carpet and buried in a garden in England. DNA fingerprinting is a technique that enables a forensic scientist to identify a person from tiny traces of blood, hair or skin.

Desalinization

Over the last three decades, desalinization has become an essential source of purified water in many parts of the world. The process is extremely efficient. Currently more than 2 billion gallons of fresh water are produced every day in the many desalinization plants to be found around the world. Desalinization is the process whereby salt is removed from saltwater using reverse osmosis, ion exchange or distillation. Desalinization is able to reduce the water content of 30,000mg/litre ionic material to 180mg/litre; a figure well above what is regarded as safe to drink.

Writing Task 2 – **Critical Analysis** – General to Specific

Hopefully, you noticed that both texts had problems with the order of information. Although writing can move in both directions – from Specific to General and from General to Specific – these examples move from General to Specific. This is a very common style of writing because it takes the reader from a more basic understanding of something to a more detailed explanation. This suits a more deductive style of writing. The Specific to General style is more suited to inductive reasoning. More information on deductive and inductive reasoning will be given on page 99.

Different sentence orders are possible but a suggested order is shown below:

DNA Fingerprinting

(Introduction) DNA fingerprinting was developed by an English geneticist by the name of Alec Jeffreys in 1983. *(Definition)* DNA fingerprinting is a technique that enables a forensic scientist to identify a person from tiny traces of blood, hair or skin. *(Explanation)* The process is very effective *(Specific Example)* and is able to indentify the linear sequence of four nucleotide bases; adenine, cytosine, guanine, and thymine present in genetic material and then match the sample to a person, living or dead. *(Specific)* DNA fingerprinting is often used to help solve murder cases *(Specific Example)* and was first used in 1986 when a skeleton was discovered ten years after being wrapped in a carpet and buried in a garden in England.

Desalinization

(General) Over the last three decades, desalinization has become an essential source of purified water in many parts of the world. *(Explanation–Definition)* Desalinization is the process whereby salt is removed from saltwater using reverse osmosis, ion exchange or distillation. *(Specific)* Currently more than 2 billion gallons of fresh water are produced every day in the many desalinization plants to be found around the world. *(Explanation)* The process is extremely efficient *(Specific Examples)* and is able to reduce the water content of 30,000mg/litre ionic material to 180mg/litre; a figure well above what is regarded as safe to drink.

Exercise
Now, look at the article extract below about energy that was written by a student and decide what you like and dislike about it. Then rewrite it.

Energy Sources

There are two advantages of using renewable energy sources. One of the benefits is that renewable energy sources are free to get because they come from weather and nature. Therefore, compared with non-renewable energy sources, it almost costs nothing to get renewable energy sources. The other merit is that renewable energy sources are pollution free. Since renewable energy sources come from nature, they won't cause environmental pollution problems and our living surroundings will be getting better.

Writing Task 2 – **Critical Analysis** – Coherence

In the previous section you were asked to analyse this article about energy written by a student.

Energy Sources

There are two advantages of using renewable energy sources. One of the benefits is that renewable energy sources are free to get because they come from weather and nature. Therefore, compared with non-renewable energy sources, it almost costs nothing to get renewable energy sources. The other merit is that renewable energy sources are pollution-free. Since renewable energy sources come from nature, they won't cause environmental pollution problems and our living surroundings will be getting better

Two of the main problems here are:

1. Unnecessary repetition of information. The article focuses on:
>   **a.** Where renewable energy comes from.
>   **b.** The fact that it costs less than more traditional forms of energy.
>   **c.** This form of energy is pollution-free.

However, each piece of information is repeated twice. Did you notice this?

2. Repeated vocabulary. The phrase **renewable energy** is repeated six times.

Possible Alternative Vocabulary	
Non-renewable energy sources	**Renewable energy sources**
traditional forms of energy coal oil gas this type of energy	alternative forms of energy solar power wind power hydroelectric power geothermal power nuclear power green energy this type of energy

One way of rewriting this is as follows:

One of the benefits of using renewable energy is that it comes from such sources as the sun, wind, and water and so, when compared with the more traditional forms of energy, costs almost nothing. The other merit is that these sources are pollution-free and would help to contribute to a much cleaner, safer environment.

Reading – Tables and Multiple Choice

Tropical Rainforests

Deforestation in the tropical areas of the world is following a course similar to the earlier clearing of the forests in Europe and North America, only advancing more rapidly. Today, more than 3 billion people live in the tropics alone, more than lived in the entire world in 1950. To provide food, wood, fuel and resources for the world's rapidly growing population, and to make room for the exploding tropical population, the world's tropical rainforests are literally disappearing.

Tropical hardwood prices continue to climb as world demand for tropical hardwoods continues to grow. A single teak log, for example, can now bring as much as $20,000. Annual world consumption of tropical hardwoods is now more than 250 million cubic meters, or over 100 billion board feet, per year. Southeast Asia until recently has been the largest source of tropical hardwoods, but that area will largely be depleted within the next five years.

All of the primary forests in India, Sri Lanka, and Bangladesh are gone and Ivory Coast's forests are essentially non-existent. Nigeria's forests have been decimated as well. As Asia's and Africa's tropical forests are depleted, consuming countries are turning increasing attention to Latin America and the Amazon, whose own rapidly growing population is also a source of pressure on the rainforests.

Also, trillions of dollars worth of oil, gas, uranium, gold, iron, bauxite and other minerals, and millions of acres of potential farm land, lie under the Amazon, the largest area of rainforest remaining on Earth. Amazon rainforests are being cleared on a vast scale for settlements, logging, gold mining, petroleum, cattle ranching, sugar cane, large hydroelectric dams, and charcoal for smelting ore. Peasant farmers also clear the rainforest to have land for planting by cutting the forest, and then in the dry season burning what they have cut.

During one month in 1995 for example, NASA satellite surveys of Brazil recorded 39,889 individual fires, up 370 percent from the same month of the prior year. In neighbouring Bolivia the smoke is sometimes so thick that schools have to close and flights have to be delayed or cancelled. Scientists estimate that until as recently as 10,000 years ago, the world had 6 billion acres of tropical rainforests. By 1950, we had a little less than 2.8 billion acres of rainforest. It was then being cut down at the rate of about 10 to 15 million acres per year.

Today we have less than 1.5 billion acres left, and we are clearing this remaining rainforest at the rate of 30 to 50 million acres per year, two to three times as rapidly as just a few decades ago. If the present rate of tropical deforestation continues, in only three decades from now, scientists anticipate that tropical rainforests will no longer exist.

One important way to help is to plant tropical hardwood trees for harvests to produce tropical hardwoods that aren't taken from the natural rainforest. It is also vitally important to get the message out to others about the importance, and the wisdom, of planting tropical hardwood trees for profit, not just because of the profit but also because of the benefit to the world.

Some countries are beginning to listen. Thailand, for example, banned logging in 1988, and Costa Rica has now protected nearly 26% of its country in national parks or reserves. The trend is unmistakable, and the facts are compelling. The world's rainforests will be either protected or they will be destroyed.

Questions 1– 4

Complete the table using **NO MORE THAN TWO WORDS OR A NUMBER.**

	10,000 years ago	Mid-20th century	Present day	Future prediction
Total Area of Rainforest left	1. .... billion acres	2. .... billion acres	3. .... billion acres	4. .... billion acres

Questions 5– 8

Choose the appropriate letter A– D.

5. One reason people are cutting down the rainforests is
    A. o make room for the growing population.
    B. to be like Europe and North America.
    C. because they need to live alone.
    D. because the rainforests are disappearing.

6. The Amazon rainforests are being decimated in order to
    A. improve tourism.
    B. raise cattle, dig mines and build dams.
    C. clear the settlements.
    D. build millions of farms.

7. Some positive changes are being made by
    A. admitting the mistakes we have made.
    B. growing trees commercially.
    C. making more profit.
    D. each country deciding what to do.

8. Why did the writer write this?
    A. To suggest different places for holiday destinations.
    B. To explain why people are so greedy.
    C. To offer possible solutions to an environmental problem.
    D. To detail the destruction of the rainforests.

Reading – YES/NO/NOT GIVEN

A Secret Well Kept

Political leaders in the days before the internet and 24-hour cable news were not subjected to the intense media scrutiny that their modern counterparts face. It was possible to rise to power and stay in office despite having skeletons in the closet that would now see one disgraced in scandal. One of the best examples of keeping damaging secrets from the public was Canadian prime minister, Lyon Mackenzie King, (almost always referred to as Mackenzie King).

Mackenzie King was born in 1874 with the proverbial silver spoon. He accumulated five university degrees, including a Ph.D. from Harvard in economics, a subject he went on to teach at that institute. In addition to being a professor and an economist, King was a lawyer and a journalist. He was also a civil servant and was appointed as Canada's first Minister of Labour. He was elected to Parliament as a Liberal and would go on to become Canada's, and the Commonwealth's, longest-serving prime minister, serving for nearly 22 years.

Mackenzie King cut his political teeth as a labour negotiator. He was successful in part because he mastered the art of conciliation. Conciliation, along with half measures, would become his trademark. "Do nothing by halves that can be done by quarters," one detractor wrote of him. And so, King sought the middle ground in order to keep the country's many factions together. He would go out of his way to avoid debate and was fond of saying, "Parliament will decide," when pressed for an answer. He was pudgy, plodding, wooden, and cold, and his speeches were slumber-inducing. Unloved, but practical and astute, he has been called Canada's greatest prime minister. He created old age pensions, unemployment insurance, and family allowance, and he left the country in much better shape than when he inherited it.

Mackenzie King died in 1950, thus passing into the mildly-interesting annals of Canadian history. Then, during the seventies, his diaries (all 30,000 pages of them) were published, and millions of Canadian jaws dropped. It turns out that King, that monotonous embodiment of Presbyterian morals, was a dedicated occultist who communicated with the dead, including his mother (who he revered), former President Roosevelt, Leonardo da Vinci, and his dogs. And he did this almost every evening for the last 25 years of his life.

King used a Ouija board and owned a crystal ball. He read tea leaves. He employed mediums and consulted a psychic. He visited palmists. He was a numerologist, always sensitive to what the numbers 7 and 17 were attempting to reveal to him. He thought that when he looked at the clock and found both hands in alignment, someone from the other side must have been watching over him. King was careful not to reveal any of his "psychical research" to the public, his departed mother having warned him that people wouldn't understand.

Adapted from a passage in: *A Sort of Homecoming – In Search of Canada* by Troy Parfitt

Questions 1– 7

Do the following questions agree with the information given in the passage? Write:

Yes   *if the statement agrees with the information*
No   *if the statement contradicts the statement information*
Not Given *if there is no information on this in the passage*

1. Mackenzie King came from a privileged background.

2. He taught economics at Harvard University.

3. He served continuously as prime minister for nearly 22 years.

4. Mackenzie King was known for his stubbornness and extreme political views.

5. His dairies were published when he was in his seventies.

6. He communicated with dead political leaders to get their advice on handling problems.

7. He regarded seeing the hands of a clock together as an auspicious sign.

Word Focus

Exercise
Match the idioms and phrases with the correct definition.

1.	have skeletons in one's closet	**A**	boring (literally "causing sleep")
2.	born with a silver spoon in one's mouth	**B**	try very hard / make an extra effort
3.	cut one's teeth	**C**	have an embarrassing secret
4.	go out of one's way (to do something)	**D**	be very surprised
5.	slumber-inducing	**E**	born into a rich and high-status family
6.	somebody's jaw dropped	**F**	learn by doing at the start of one's career

Reading – Short Answers and Sentence Completion

The Halifax Explosion

Before the atomic bomb was dropped on Hiroshima in 1945, the largest-ever non-natural explosion had taken place in 1917 in the eastern Canadian port city of Halifax. With the outbreak of World War I, Halifax was effectively transformed into a boomtown. Convoys gathered weekly in Bedford Basin (the north-western end of Halifax Harbour) in order to traverse the Atlantic, and Halifax Harbour became heavy with vessels of one variety or another. This spike in boat traffic was not dealt with efficiently and collisions became almost normal.

On December 1st, 1917, the French vessel *Mont Blanc* left New York in order to join a convoy in Halifax after being loaded with 226,797 kilograms of TNT (an explosive), 223,188 kilograms of benzol (a type of gasoline), 1,602,519 kilograms of wet picric acid (an explosive), and 544,311 kilograms of dry picric acid (another explosive). On December 6th, the *Mont Blanc* was ushered into Halifax's harbour after the U-boat nets had been raised.

At the same time, the cargoless Norwegian ship, *Imo*, left Bedford Basin en route to New York in order to pick up relief items for transport to war-torn Belgium. *Imo* was behind schedule and attempting to remedy that. She passed a boat on the wrong side before sending a tugboat retreating to port. By the time she reached the Narrows, she was in the wrong channel and going too fast. The *Mont Blanc* sounded her whistle, but the *Imo* sounded back twice, refusing to alter course. At the last moment, the *Mont Blanc* veered and the *Imo* reversed, but it was too late. From the gash formed in the French boat's hull seeped a noxious spiral of oily, orange-dappled smoke. *Mont Blanc*'s crew rowed to shore on the Dartmouth side, but no one could decipher their warnings. Their fiery vessel then casually drifted toward the Halifax side where it came to rest against one of the piers.

This spectacle drew thousands of onlookers. People crowded docks and windows filled with curious faces. As many as 1,600 died instantly when the boat exploded. Around 9,000 were injured, 6,000 seriously so. Approximately 12,000 buildings were severely damaged; virtually every building in town was damaged to some extent; 1,630 were rendered nonexistent. Around 6,000 people were made homeless and 25,000 people (half the population) were left without suitable housing.

The Halifax Explosion, as it became known, was the largest manmade detonation to date, approximately one fifth the ferocity of the bomb later dropped on Hiroshima. It sent up a column of smoke reckoned to be 7,000 metres in height. It was felt more than 480 kilometres away. It flung a ship gun barrel some 5.5 kilometres, and part of an anchor, which weighed 517 kilograms, around 3 kilometres. The blast absolutely flattened a district known as Richmond. It also caused a tsunami that saw a wave 18 metres above the high-water mark deposit the *Imo* onto the shore of the Dartmouth side. The pressure wave of air that was produced snapped trees, bent iron rails, and grounded ships. That evening, a blizzard commenced and it would continue until the next day, leaving 40 centimetres of snow in its wake. Consequently, many of those trapped within collapsed structures died of exposure. Historians put the death toll of the Halifax Explosion at approximately 2,000.

Adapted from a passage in: *A Sort of Homecoming – In Search of Canada* by Troy Parfitt

Questions 1–5

Answer these questions using NO MORE THAN THREE WORDS.

1. What cargo was the *Mont Blanc* carrying?

2. What was the final intended destination of the *Imo*?

3. How many people were living in Halifax at that time of the explosion?

4. How high was the tsunami that was caused by the explosion?

5. What was the total number of fatalities?

Questions 6–10

Complete the sentences using NO MORE THAN THREE WORDS.

6. During World War One, Halifax Harbour was unable to properly handle the increased shipping traffic and there were numerous _____.

7. The *Imo* was not in the correct _____ and travelling too fast.

8. _____ of people were watching the burning ship when it exploded.

9. The Halifax Explosion had about _____ of the power of the Hiroshima bomb.

10. Freezing weather brought by a blizzard caused the death of some survivors who were _____ under collapsed buildings.

Writing Task 2 – **Sample Essay** – Coherence

Exercise
Try to put the words and phrases below in the correct place in the Task 2. essay

Indeed	In fact
I feel, however, that	The argument against studying in a foreign country mainly focuses on the fact that
In addition	To conclude
In addition	While it is true that a certain degree of sacrifice is needed

Task 2
Discuss the advantages and disadvantages of studying overseas and then give your opinion.

With the world becoming more and more like a global village, and with economies improving, many people have the opportunity to study abroad. Seen by many as a way to improve a second language, experience a foreign culture and come back home with a qualification, others regard it as a waste of time and money. **1.** .... the advantages far outweigh the disadvantages when studying abroad.

2. .... it costs a lot of money and it causes a huge upheaval for not only the students but also their family and friends. **3.** .... for many, they are spending their life savings in order to experience one year abroad. **4.** ...., there is no guarantee that when they return home after their studies a job will be waiting for them.

5. ...., the idea that this is nothing more than a complete waste of money and will only result in unemployment is clearly untrue. From an academic point of view, the chance to broaden your knowledge and experience new ideas and concepts can only be seen as positive. It is also essential for people keen on furthering their career and enhancing their chances of promotion.

6. ...., the chance to hone interpersonal skills, develop a more international outlook on life as well as have the opportunity to become more independent are priceless experiences that will benefit you for the rest of your life. **7.** ...., this is an ideal way to create self-confidence and a sense of purpose in the student that is hard to develop in any other way.

8. ...., studying overseas offers a student a chance of a lifetime both academically and personally. It will help them keep one step ahead of the competition when finding work as well as provide them with the chance to become a more rounded, mature person.

Writing Task 2 – **Cause and Effect**

When writing problem/solution essays you have to write about:

> **1.** the cause of the problem
> **2.** the effect of the problem
> **3.** the solution of the problem - focus on reducing/eliminating the cause NOT the effect

It is important to write about the effects of the problem in the introduction because this creates the topic importance for your essay. The effects, on the other hand, are only the symptoms of the real problem. If you can eliminate the causes of stress, there will be no symptoms to worry about.

However, many students give solutions for eliminating the effects of a problem but fail to resolve the real issue which is, "How can you help solve the problem?" This means you must focus on, for instance, the cause of the increasing stress in society and not the headaches and sleepless nights it causes. The examiner is not interested in hearing about how you go home at night and listen to music while drinking a glass of red wine after a long soak in a bath! Like all Task 2 essays, the topics are very general and must be developed accordingly.

Are the following sentences describing a **SOLUTION** for an **EFFECT** or a **CAUSE**? Write **E** or **C**.

Global Warming

1. We will need to build sea walls to protect coastal properties.

2. Governments should subsidize public transportation.

Childhood Obesity

1. There should be a ban on advertisements for junk food.

2. Children need to be screened for diabetes.

Bullying in Schools

1. Schools should provide free counselling sessions for the victims of bullying.

2. Teachers have to try harder to create a class atmosphere of inclusion.

Writing Task 2 – Cause and Effect

Exercise
Now look at the text about global warming and complete the flow chart below by writing the correct piece of information in the right numbered box.

The dramatic increase in global warming can be attributed to one main factor, the increase in CO_2 in the atmosphere. This was brought about by three main causes. The first was an increase in industrialization which led to an increase in the production of electricity. The second cause was a rise in transportation which resulted from better infrastructure. The final cause was deforestation which was largely due to an unprecedented demand for more land because of the need to grow biofuels and build residential homes.

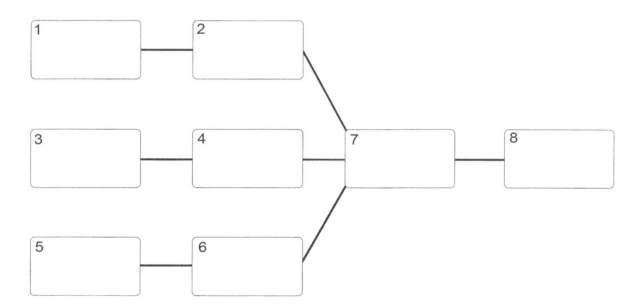

Writing Task 2 – **Writing the Essay** – Advantages and Disadvantages

Task 2.
Zoos are often seen as important but poor alternatives to allowing animals to remain in their natural environment. Discuss the advantages and disadvantages of keeping animals in captivity and then give your opinion.

Step 1 ....   Read the Task 2 instructions carefully

Step 2 ....   Decide which type of essay it is – Type **A**, **B**, or **C**   (see page 48)

Step 3 ....   Understand the topic

Step 4............   Select your topic importance

> **a.** background information
> **b.** what people / groups are interested?
> **c.** what is changing in society?

Step 5 ....   Select your topic direction (are there more advantages or disadvantages?)

Step 6 ....   Main Body; use one or more of the brainstorming techniques shown on page 53 and list points on both sides of the argument

Advantages	Disadvantages

Exercise
Now write your essay using a four-paragraph structure.

Remember: you must include opinions for both advantages and disadvantages in order to make your essay balanced.

Writing Task 2 – **Critical Analysis** – Self-Analysis

As mentioned earlier on, it is very important to develop the ability to self-correct. In other words, are you able to critically analyse what you have written? Many students say, "If I could analyse my writing I wouldn't make the mistakes in the first place." However, is this really true? Think of the number of times you have made mistakes when speaking and then self-corrected. You can make mistakes and know that you have made one.

What is important is to have a mental checklist of what to look for. By now you should have a better idea of the kind of mistakes that can be made.

Exercise
Look at the four paragraphs below. Each paragraph was written by a different student about whether or not universities should only focus on the knowledge and skills needed in the workplace. Read each paragraph and then, by using the criteria below, decide what is wrong with the bold/underlined words or phrases.

Self-correction check list

1.	informal / formal style	**6.**	illogical / logical
2.	too many short sentences	**7.**	general to specific
3.	repeated information	**8.**	grammar
4.	repeated vocabulary	**9.**	spelling
5.	development of ideas	**10.**	higher level vocabulary

A
(Also think about the logic of this sentence)
To conclude, I believe that a university that produces competent graduates with **properly** knowledge and skills for the workplace are more effective and efficient whatever **tasks given** to them.

B
In conclusion, universities should focus on **providing students in-depth knowledge** accompanied by appropriate skills in line with the **carer** they decide to take. Although providing more information would be practical **yet** expertise in a particular field would tend to matter more.

C
In conclusion, universities need to make changes to the subjects and courses on offer to allow **student** to learn directly the knowledge and skills **need** for a better **career life**. Hopefully, this move will **increase** the percentage of jobless citizens in the world today.

D
To conclude, from my personal **points** of view, universities should impart **its** knowledge and practical skills, that are relevant in the workplace because, with more **knowledge and skills students** will adjust quickly in **his** new job.

Writing Task 2 – Sample Problem and Solution Essay

Exercise
Try to put the words and phrases below in the correct place in the Task 2 essay.

With this in mind	for example
Many scholars are now convinced	All in all, I am firmly convinced
Another way to help address this problem would be if	The first recommendation would be to provide
In addition	Finally
Indeed	therefore

Task 2
A rapidly increasing global population will lead to many social and environmental problems unless something is done to help control this impending catastrophe. Suggest ways to help slow down this trend.

1. .... future wars will be triggered by a lack of land, food and water rather than for political reasons. One of the main causes of this is likely to be the global population explosion. It is 2. .... essential that ways to help control this are put into action before it is too late. 3. .... several suggestions to help make inroads into this phenomenon are offered in the following article.

4. .... tax-incentives for parents who do not exceed the stated maximum number of children. A government could 5. .... encourage families to only have one child by keeping their salary tax at a basic level. This would immediately increase (perhaps even double) if they had a second child.

6. .... the government could introduce sex education lessons into the national curriculum and establish family planning clinics in the more rural areas of the country. 7. .... free contraceptives could be distributed to low-income households if they attended a series of lessons on family planning.

8. .... the introduction of a welfare system to ease the financial burden of the poorer families in both urban and rural areas would also help. 9. .... as families began to realize that less children means more money and a better lifestyle, they would be further encouraged to use contraception.

10. .... we will be able combat this problem effectively with the intervention of the appropriate authorities and the implementation of tax incentives and the all-important development of family planning education. It is only by taking such actions that it becomes possible to develop and then maintain a high quality of life, a healthy environment and a sound economy in every country in the world.

Writing Task 2 – Conclusions

A conclusion allows your essay to come full circle by restating your topic direction. If you start off agreeing with the opinion in the Task 2 statement and end by disagreeing, you have written an essay that is completely illogical and your grade will be lowered. It is perfectly acceptable to add information from the middle three paragraphs but DO NOT add any new ideas or examples. Remember: in the conclusion you are only confirming what you have already said. Also, using the same wording that you have already used is simply copying from other paragraphs; use a different word order and synonyms to create a new sentence structure.

Exercise
Read an introduction about *'fame versus privacy'* and then decide which conclusion – **A**, **B**, **C**, **D** – best suits the introduction.

Introduction

A common childhood dream is to become a famous movie star or TV personality. Yet, those who achieve such an ambition often complain bitterly about the invasion of their privacy by the media. In my opinion there is no cause for complaint as being in the public eye is part of being famous.

A. In conclusion, although it can't be very nice being followed by lots of people, nobody asked them to be famous. If I were famous, I would think that I was very lucky and would enjoy everything about being famous.

B. All in all, people in the entertainment business have to accept that being in the public eye is part of being famous and so they have no reason to complain.

C. To conclude, anyone wanting to be famous must accept the inevitable curiosity from the public and realise that fame comes with a price to pay – the loss of your right to privacy.

D. To sum up, the paparazzi make life very difficult for lots of people. I can't imagine what life would be like. I'm glad that I'm not famous.

Exercise
Now, write an introduction and conclusion for the following Task 2 question.

Travelling abroad on holiday can be fun and a unique learning experience. However, many people do not know their own country. How can we encourage people to vacation at home?

Writing Task 2 – **Writing The Essay** – Conclusions

Writing conclusions often presents a problem for students. To help make this process a little easier it is useful to look at a checklist of points that need to be considered. Tick **YES** or **NO** in the columns to the right of the table depending on which action you think needs to be taken.

		YES	NO
1.	Include the conclusion as the last part of the main body		
2.	Use the conclusion to create a feeling of wanting to know more		
3.	Restate the topic direction		
4.	Put extra information or evidence to support your ideas into the conclusion		
5.	The conclusion should summarize the main body		
6.	Start the conclusion by writing, "In conclusion"		
7.	Put the conclusion in the last paragraph		

Read the main body for an essay on the topic of two-tier pricing for tourists, and then read the two conclusions that follow. Now decide which conclusion best fits the main body.

BODY

A strong argument for double-pricing is that local people pay taxes that are spent on museums, national parks and other facilities. Therefore, they deserve to pay lower admission charges. If local people have to pay the same admission charges as foreign tourists, they would, in effect, be paying more. Asking foreigners to pay more for subsidised sectors is actually commonplace around the world. Most countries, for example, require foreign students to pay much higher tuition fees than local residents.

Another reason often given to justify charging foreigners more is that there is no other way to raise money. Many poor countries have insufficient funds for even basic services like health care and education. They do not have money for cultural, historical, and environmental attractions. These are luxuries that they cannot afford. Without the extra money from double-pricing, historical sites in poor countries would be unable to protect these cultural treasures. Likewise, national parks would have insufficient resources to protect the flora and fauna.

Critics of double-pricing claim that charging tourists more is simply morally wrong. There is some truth that it can be unfair but as mentioned above locals have in many cases already contributed by paying taxes. Furthermore, although an irritation for foreign tourists, they can afford to pay more than the average local person, and the inflated prices are usually still low. If the local people were asked to pay the same higher fees, most of them would be unable to enjoy their own national attractions.

CONCLUSION 1

All in all, I believe that double-pricing is justifiable because local people pay taxes that are spent on museums, national parks and other facilities so they deserve to pay lower admission charges. In addition, there is no other way to raise money, and foreign tourists can afford to pay more. For example, if you visit a historical site in Thailand and need to pay a higher admission than a local person, then you might be angry, but you can afford it, and they need the money to keep the place in good condition.

CONCLUSION 2

All in all, although charging higher prices to foreigners seems unfair, I believe that this double-pricing can be justified in some circumstances. Local people have already contributed to facilities through paying taxes, and the authorities have few alternatives for raising money to maintain attractions.

Writing Task 2 – Developing a Logical Argument

Simply writing in a formal style doesn't mean that your essay is well written. Many other things need to be considered before you can truly say, "I can write well in English."

One very important skill to learn is the development of a logical argument. Think of this as the ability to support your opinion with enough information to convince other people that your viewpoint is justified. The ideas that support your opinion must be clearly detailed and placed in a logical order.

Imagine if you presented an opinion that states:

I firmly believe that recessions can lead to the development of a stronger police force.

As supporting information you then go on to say:

Evidence of this is an increase in crime following a fall in the country's economy.

Do you think that this supporting idea has fully explained the thinking behind your opinion? Does anything seem to be missing? Would you add any extra information to create a better sense of completeness to this argument?

The main problem here is that the development of the argument, leading to the conclusion that a recession can lead to a stronger police force, is incomplete. The argument would be seen by the examiner as a weak argument because the supporting points do not bring the reader to the same conclusion as the writer. A better development of ideas would have been:

I firmly believe that recessions can lead to the development of a stronger police force. Evidence of this is an increase in crime following an inevitable rise in unemployment. As this situation escalates, and society becomes more unstable, greater numbers of police are needed to help restore order to society.

The paragraph above offers only an overview of the topic but, nevertheless, develops the argument more fully and in a logical step by step approach. As seen earlier, logic is essential for both the presentation and content of your essay and needs time to develop.

Many people assume that logic is an absolute truth, that logic cannot be denied, and that logic is universal and, therefore, obvious. However, when we think about how logic develops we can see that the way we think, the way we explain things is influenced, perhaps determined, by the culture we grow up in. On the following page is an extract from an article written by Tatsuo Motokawa from the Tokyo Institute of Technology about the differences in logic he has observed between the West and the East. The diagrams below represent the way Western people and Asian people think. Which is which?

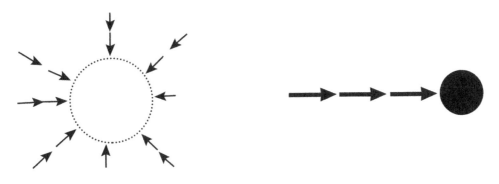

Writing Task 2 – Developing a Logical Argument

An extract from Sushi Science and Hamburger Science

By

Tatsuo Motokawa

Tokyo Institute of Technology

When you Western people read the papers written by Japanese scientists, you will often have difficulties in understanding what the authors wanted to say, even if the article is written in English. One obvious cause is poor English; another cause is the difference in "logic." Western logic is quite clear: it has a structure in which each statement is tightly connected and linearly arranged to reach a conclusion. Japanese logic is not so clear. Westerners may well find no logic at all. Japanese people talk about something and, without stating a conclusion, move the discussion to another topic. These two topics often have no logical connection, although they are related in the mind of Japanese people. What Japanese are trying to do is to describe one fact from various points of view. Each view is connected by imagery to others, not by strict logic such as syllogism.

Linear logic is very effective: it illuminates one side of the fact clearly. But that's all. Japanese logic is like a net that embraces one fact, and thus it makes up a hollow, three-dimensional structure. The net is not strongly woven and, of course, the net is leaky. It is not a clear rigid logic that binds up the fact. Rather, the net creates an atmosphere that vaguely surrounds the fact. This is another example of the "one-many" difference. Westerners prefer the one fixed point of view, while Easterners prefer the multiple points of view. This can also be interpreted as an example of "I - no I" difference because one fixed point in the West is "I".

The important difference between the two languages is that the Japanese people do not state a conclusion. What they do is just point at some direction. This, I guess, is what annoys Western people most. If you state no conclusion, it is the same thing as saying nothing. But wait. Japanese people think like this: if we state a conclusion, it means that our statement is the truth. Such a statement is definitely false because our words can never be absolutely true. In addition to that, if we state a conclusion, we close our world. If we do not state a conclusion and let other people draw the conclusion by themselves, our world is open to others. If other people come to the same conclusion as the one we have in mind, then we can share the conclusion and we are happy in harmony. If other people do not come to the same conclusion, we just wait. We do not push our conclusion on other people; this is the way we keep our harmony. Aggressiveness is no virtue in the East.

The closed system is a noted characteristic of Western science. Every scientist makes his own world and closes it to other people. What others can do is either to become a believer of that dogma or to destroy it and build up a new one of their own. There is always a fight between two closed systems.

Remember: although this essay focuses on Japanese people, many other Asians think in a similar way, in part because of a Confucian and/or Buddhist background.

Writing Task 2 – **Logical Arguments** – Inductive/Deductive Reasoning

Although there are as many arguments as people, there are two basic styles of arguing – **deductive** and **inductive** reasoning. While the definitions given below are actually wider than suggested here, you will still be able to see that the way you develop your thinking can follow different paths of logic.

Deductive

Deductive reasoning is when information flows from general to specific. For instance:

> Everyone who speaks English is British.
> Yoshi speaks English.
> Therefore, Yoshi is British

This deductive argument is valid and, therefore, logical because the conclusion you must reach is that Yoshi is British. However, the premise – or general observation – that everyone who speaks English is British is false.

If all of the premises are true then by deductive reasoning or logic, we can say that the conclusion is 100% true. Information expressed deductively is based on laws, rules and accepted principles. Can you think of an example of deductive reasoning?

Deductive logic can be seen as offering no new information but rather expressing more clearly what is stated often implicitly, in the premises. This form of logic is built up in a step like progression and is used mainly in mathematics.

Inductive

Inductive reasoning is when information flows from specific to general. For instance:

> I have seen many insects.
> All of these insects could fly.
> Therefore, all insects can probably fly.

If all of the premises are true then by inductive reasoning or logic, we can say that the conclusion is *probably* true. Information expressed inductively is based on experience but depends on further observation, analysis, inference and further testing. Can you think of an example of inductive reasoning?

Inductive logic, on the other hand, does offer new, inferred information even if the certainty of its truth is limited. This form of logic is used for most other fields of research.

At this stage in the development of your writing skills, the main point to learn here is that we can be thinking logically, we can be developing ideas step by step but our conclusion is still wrong or our argument too weak because of the premises we add.

IELTS IS TAUGHT IN JAPAN
I TEACH IELTS
I AM JAPANESE
THEREFORE, DO I LIVE IN JAPAN ?

Spider Map

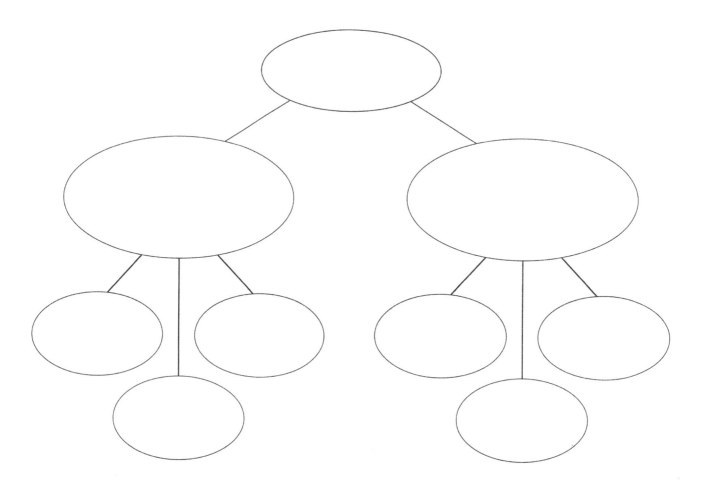

ANSWERS

Page 7

	2003	2004	2005
University A	6	8	6
University B	4	4	6

Page 8

The best introduction is 3. The other introductory sentences have multiple problems including: (1) "the number of coffee" and "7-year period" are wrong. (2) Doesn't mention consumption of coffee, or give a time reference. (4) Uses the word "below".

Page 9
The number of …..
accidents, children, students

The amount of …..
coffee, electricity, free time, income, pollution

The levels of …..
life expectancy, income, pollution

The table provides data on changes in the levels of population growth in four different cities over an 11-year period from 1997 to 2007.

The bar chart highlights information on changes in the levels of Internet usage in six different states in America over a 19-year period from 1985 to 2003.

Page 10
In general, University A had more staff over this period of time than University B.

Page 11

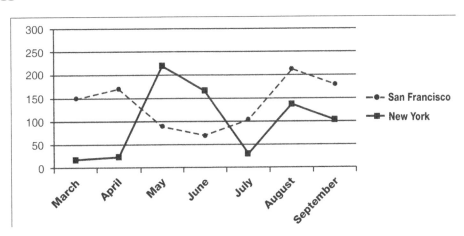

The line chart provides information on changes in the amount of pollen in San Francisco and New York over 7 months from March to September in 2012.

Generally speaking, pollen levels rose in both cities over this period of time.

Page 12
1. B 2. C 3. B 4. C

1.
Despite sales falling in New York from US$165,000 in 2003 to US$132,000, figures remained higher than all of the other five cities.

2.

The percentage of women majoring in science subjects increased slightly from 7% to 8% over this period of time.

3.

Levels of pollution rose dramatically from 1200 metric tons in 2007 to 3000 metric tons in 2010, a climb of 1800 metric tons.

4.

The number of accidents in school playgrounds fell by 15% over the five years, decreasing substantially from 27% to 12%.

5.

Travelling by bus also dropped with the total mileage falling from 540,000 miles in 2001 to 235,000 miles 7 years later.

6.

Generally speaking, salaries were significantly higher in Europe than in Asia.

Page 15
1. D 2. B 3. D 4. C 5. D

Page 16
C D F (any order)

Page 17
The table compares and contrasts data on migration to and from the United Kingdom over an 8-year period from 2002 to 2009.

General Statement Trend
Generally speaking, migration both into and out of the country increased over this period of time.

General Statement Main Idea
An overview of the diagram shows that, figures for migration into the country were always higher than for those out of the United Kingdom.

Units
9,500 radios,   885,000 vehicles,   79.6 million viewers a day,   15,300 flights,   56% / 56 per cent / 56 percent, US$6,870

Note that both 'per cent' and 'percent' are correct. 'Per cent' is usually used in British English and 'percent' is more common in American English. You can use either form; the important thing is to be consistent.

Page 18
The line chart provides data on the changes in university admissions from Nepal in the United Kingdom over a 10-year period from 1995 to 2004.

Generally speaking, despite obvious fluctuations, admissions increased slightly over this period of time.

More specifically, university admissions were exactly 300 in 1995. This was followed by a continued rise in figures to exactly 400 in 1997, an increase of 100 students. Numbers then fell to just under 300 in 1998 and a little less than 100 in 1999. A further decrease was experienced in the following year with admissions settling at approximately 75. However, by 2002 the number of students going to the UK had risen to slightly less than 400 in 2002. The following year saw a dramatic drop in figures to almost zero admissions but figures then recovered in 2004 with almost 400 Nepalese students entering the UK to study.

Page 19
The table shows information on participation levels of men and women in seven activities over three age groups.

Main body with underlined phrases for male and female
The least preferred activity for males in the 36-45 age group was meditation with 3% participation whereas 12% of all females surveyed did this activity. The biggest overall increase in percentage in any activity for women was for yoga which rose from 7% in the youngest age group to 42% in the oldest age group. The opposite sex, however,

experienced the biggest change in fishing from 12% to 45% respectively, a total climb of 33%. No change was seen in jogging at 31% in the two older age groups for <u>women</u>. Similarly, their <u>counterparts</u> saw no variation for yoga which remained at 7% in the same two age groups. It is interesting to note that the biggest difference between the <u>two sexes</u> in any one age group and the same activity was for baseball in the youngest age group; <u>men</u> had 87% whilst the <u>opposite gender</u> had only 2%.

Reducing Main Body
The final sentence in the main body could be removed because of the opening phrase - *It is interesting to note that*. No opinions can be added to Task 1 writing and doing so can lead to a lowering of your final grade.

Also, the first sentence could be removed as this is not so important. It mentions that participation in meditation was 3% for men in the 36-45 age group but this is not the smallest overall figure for men in this activity. The 21-35 age group has zero participants and is actually the lowest figure for any activity for men.

Page 20 - (some examples)
The figure for 2010 is the largest and that for 2001 is the smallest.
The figure for 2005 is exactly half that for 2010.
The figure for 2008 is exactly double that for 2004.
The figure for 2001 is exactly a third that for 2003.
The figure for 2002 is exactly a quarter that for 2008.

Page 21
The bar chart provides data on the number of papers taken for publication from Warwick University's Engineering Faculty for the 12 months of 2011. Despite fluctuations and a notable peak in July, there was an overall downward trend during the year.

In January there were about 27 papers accepted for publication; this was the second highest number for the year. The following month there were only 11 papers taken. That figure rose to 24 in March but then fell again over the next two months. From 13 papers in May the number rose sharply to a yearly peak of 44 papers in July.

In August, only 15 papers were accepted, a little more than a third of the total for the previous month. Over the last four months of the year, the number of accepted papers remained below the August figure, reaching a yearly low in November with 6 papers.

Page 22

	Key Features	Time Period	No Time Period
1.	The extremes (the biggest and the smallest)	YES	YES
2.	The constant (no change)	YES	NO
3.	The longest continued rise / fall over a period of time	YES	NO
4.	The only category to always rise / fall	YES	NO
5.	A peak	YES	NO
6.	A trough	YES	NO
7.	Biggest or smallest increase / Biggest or smallest decrease	YES	NO
8.	Two categories the same / two points the same in one category	YES	YES
9.	Comparison between two categories	YES	YES

1 E   2 G   3 I   4 B   5 A   6 F   7 H   8 C   9 D

Page 24
1. D   2. G   3. A   4. F   5. E   6. C

Page 26

1. marine plains / salt lakes   2. rain   3. wind   (any order for 2. and 3.)   4. evaporation   5. transpiration   (any order for 4. and 5.)   6. the root zone   7. land use / people   8. irrigation   9. dryland   (any order for 8. and 9.)   10. mobilizing salt   11. land use   12. clearing native vegetation / broad acre farming / grazing   13. the soil surface / surface water bodies

Page 27

The bar chart shows information on the changes in the number of miles travelled by three different salesmen over a 6-month period in 2010.

<u>General Statement Trend</u>

Overall, mileage increased for both salesman A and B but, despite clear fluctuations, salesman C had the same figures in January and June.

<u>General Statement Main Idea</u>

In general, salesman B tended to travel more miles than either salesman A or salesman C over this time period.

1.   The furthest distance travelled was in June by salesman B with a mileage of slightly under 11,000 miles.

2.   The biggest decrease was from a little under 10,000 miles in February to just under 2,500 in April by salesman A.

3.   The largest peak for salesman A was in February with a figure of a little over 10,000 miles.

4.   The lowest trough was also for salesman A when figures fell to a little under 2,500 miles in April.

5.   In January, mileage for both salesman A and C were exactly the same at slightly more than 5,000.

6.   The smallest decrease over two consecutive months was for salesman C with the distance travelled falling from exactly 7,500 miles to slightly less than 7,500.

Page 28

Best order - 2 A   4 B   1 C   3 D

Page 30

1. on   2. in   3. of   4. in / at / for   5. with   6. in   7. at   8. at   9. from

We cannot write about "more women" or "fewer women" from any of the countries because we only know the percentage of women in tertiary education. We do not know how many women there are and so we can only talk about higher or lower percentages. The population in each county will be different and so, for example, 57.2% in 2005 for the US and UK will not be the same number of women.

NOTE: You cannot add your opinions, or interpretation of why you think something happened, to a Task 1 essay. The only exception is when you are writing about a map that shows several possible locations for a new building. For this you have to discuss the advantages and disadvantages of each potential site.

Page 31

1. on   2. in   3. of   4. by   5. in   6. in   7. on   8. in   9. of   10. for   11. for   12. on   13. on   14. on   15. under   16. on   17. by   18. on   19. by   20. in   21. of

Page 32

<u>Introduction</u>

Do not refer to the diagram as a 'picture'. It is important to try and add extra information from the diagram.

<u>General Statement</u>

The general statement is far too general. There is no time period and so it is not possible to refer to a trend. However, you can write about the biggest and smallest percentages – Italy and Brazil respectively. Instead of writing "2011" again, you could write – "in this particular year."

<u>Main Body</u>

General knowledge is also included. For instance, "their country is close politically to Libya," "this is not enough for them" and, "which is strange … they are near Libya on the map." It is also not correct to refer to the diagram as a "picture" – "illustration" would be better. The reference to other countries in Europe is followed by the whole list stated at the bottom of the diagram. Long lists – anything over four categories – is usually seen by the examiner as too many.

Page 35
1. repeated movements   2. unusual posture   3. Satchmo syndrome   4. Men, female musicians
5. Glenn Gould   6. stage diving / crowd surfing   7. dying

Page 36
1. E   2. H   3. C   4. G

Page 37
1. on   2. in   3. on / in   4. of   5. on / toward (s) / for   6. of   7. on   8. on / toward (s) / for   9. by   10. for / to
11. on   12. with   13. for / of   14. of

Page 40
The illustration details the various stages involved in the creation of graphics from a customer's description of his artwork.

First of all, the customer talks to the graphic artist about his artwork and describes what he wants. The artist then creates the graphics using the information that he has been given. The finished graphics are subsequently reviewed by a reviewer to see how good they are. After this, if it is felt that they do not look very good, they go back to the graphic artist who redesigns them. If, however, the graphics pass the standards set by the company, they are passed to the client who will either approve or reject them. If they are considered unacceptable they go back to the designer. However, if the graphics are to the client's liking, they will be approved and saved in their database. Once the graphics have been stored in the company's data base, they are sent to the customer.

1. is harvested   2. is boiled, is added   3. is shaken   4. are cut, they are transported   5. is written

Page 41
The illustration provided details of the various stages involved in the registration of a student into a faculty.

To start this process a prospective student must submit his or her registration form to the administration department in the college. Once this has been done, the form is subsequently checked to see if it has been done correctly. If it hasn't, then it is returned to the student who must then amend the form. Registration forms that are acknowledged as being complete are then passed onto the registrar who determines whether or not the student meets the minimum standards. Failure to meet these standards results in a rejection letter being written and sent to the student. If the letter meets the minimum standard then the faculty advisor must decide if the applicant is suitable for the program. An affirmative results in an acceptance letter being written and then sent to the student. If considered unacceptable, the advisor writes a rejection letter which is then sent.

Page 42
The map presented here highlights the changes that have occurred in Boracay, turning from a small, undeveloped island to a tourist focused destination over a 40-year period from 1970 to 2010.

The caves on the northern coast of the island were closed to the public and the fish market on the west coast was closed to make way for restaurants, bars and a sailing club. Wind surfing and diving schools have been developed on the opposite coast from a once deserted area.

The beach huts on the southern part of the island have gone and been replaced with a hotel beach resort. The white, sandy beach was destroyed by a typhoon and the sand dunes are now home to diving schools and cottages. The original footpath, leading from the caves has been turned into a road that runs the length of the island and connects all of the main tourist spots.

Page 45
1. foraging   2. hunting (1. and 2. in any order)   3. labourers   4. farms   5. factories   6. a century ago   7. parts
8. systems   9. radical   10. extraction   11. diabetes   12. humans

Page 46
1. harmony   2. contrast   (answers 1. and 2. in any order)   3. waterborne   4. Chinese   5. chilies

6./7. Portuguese, Dutch, French, Japanese (any two)   8./9. ghee, coconut oil   (in this order) or dairy products, coconut milk   (in this order) 10. longer

Page 47
ACROSS 1. society   2. culture   3. environment   4. education   5. ecology
DOWN 1. health   2. technology   3. tourism   4. globalization

Page 48
1. C   2. A   3. B

Page 49
1. B - Introduction   2. B - Conclusion   3. C - Main Body or A - Introduction   4. A - Conclusion
5. A - Introduction

You should need approximately 12 to 15 sentences for a 250-word essay.

Page 50
Global warming is seen as a great problem throughout the world. Although the individual might find it difficult to do anything about this, many countries like America and the United Kingdom are passing regulations to help by means of such actions as monitoring carbon dioxide emissions more carefully. As this trend continues and other countries begin to encourage people to use public transport, the ability to reverse this trend will become easier.

Page 51
1. Many scientists see a direct link between carbon dioxide and global warming.

(When you discuss your ideas or data at university you should write with caution rather than assertion. In other words, avoid using words like: 'clearly', 'obviously', 'without a doubt', 'undoubtedly', 'definitely' and so on. The reason for this is that when you do research you must take into consideration that you might not have all of the necessary data to make the absolute claims you are making. This is called hedging. The words 'suggest', 'seemingly', 'unlikely', 'might' and 'indicate' are often used in hedging.)

2. It might be possible to reduce inner city pollution by encouraging car owners to use public transport.
(You must not use contractions - 'It's' - and you must hedge. See question 1 above.)

3. The government could, for example, spend less money on developing coal mines and more on finding alternative sources of energy.
(It is usually considered informal to ask questions.)

4. The main benefit is that speaking another language allows you to travel more easily in a foreign country.
(Starting a sentence with 'The first advantage' is not wrong but it certainly lacks creativity. Try to find other ways to write - First, Second, Third - by using phrases like: 'The main benefit', The greatest advantage' and so on.)

5. It is important to consider how better relationships between countries can be encouraged.
(Direct references to people are often seen as too informal when writing at university. This varies from professor to professor but it is, nevertheless, a good skill to learn and makes your writing more formal and your skills in writing more flexible.)

6. Daily life is influenced by a number of factors.
(Direct references to people - 'our' - are often seen as too informal when writing at university.)

7. Japanese people tend to do things in a certain style.
(The expression, 'We, Japanese' is seen as too informal. It is much better to use a more indirect style of referring to Japanese people.)

8. Many things can be done to help poor people.
(Direct references to people - 'We' - are often seen as too informal when writing at university.)

9. Ten children were awarded sponsorships to attend a private school.
(Do not start a sentence using figures; these should be written. Also, the word - 'kids' - is too informal and the phrase - 'were given away to study' - is less formal than - 'were awarded sponsorships'.)

1. Assistance   2. discovery   3. provision   4. prevention

Page 52
1. serious   2. precise   3. analytical   4. rational   5. impersonal   6. hedged   7. intellectual   8. objective
9. formal

Currently, a significant number of men are unemployed in Afghanistan. However, before the late 20th century it was normal to work with their siblings on their family farm. There appears to be various reasons for this social phenomenon but one key factor, the result of financial pressures, is a significant migration toward cities. There are mixed views about the effects of this change and its possible influence on their customs and traditions. It has been stated that a number of problems may develop such as the decreasing size of the farming communities as well as the loss of their traditions. There seems to be considerable evidence to support his views and there may be an argument in favour of requesting sponsorship from the government to assist these farmers.

NOTE: many students like to uses phrases like - 'According to an article in the Los Angeles Times', 'Research conducted in Tokyo University'. These are not seen by IELTS examiners as an appropriate style for this type of essay. At university you would be expected to reference your information by stating more clearly where your data came from, but for IELTS you do not have to do this. Adding information about various studies or research is seen as an attempt to standardize your writing by remembering certain phrases or sentences and then adding them, perhaps with minor changes, to every essay.

Informal	Formal
These days	Currently
A lot of	A significant number of
Guys	Men
Brothers and sisters	Siblings
Why is this?	There appear to be several reasons for this
One thing	One key factor
Loads of people have moved	Significant / Appreciable migration
Money problems	Financial pressures
Is this good for society?	There are mixed views about the effects ...
Jones has studied this	Jones (2007) states that ...
There is no doubt that	There is considerable evidence to ...
Ask	Requesting
Giving money	Sponsorship
To help	To assist

Page 53
THINK - CREATE - DEVELOP
The reasons leading to crime
There are many reasons that can lead to someone committing a crime but common reasons are - poverty, inequality, abuse, drug use, teenage pregnancies.

What problems crime might cause
The fear of crime can deeply affect society. While this fear can affect people in different ways, it is usually the media that focuses our attention on certain groups of people in society. Schools become more security conscious and children will be escorted to school. Elderly people will stay at home more and so become more isolated from society.

The advantages of logging
It provides more room for housing and businesses which in turn creates more employment. It also provides building material for the construction business, as well as trees for the paper business.

The disadvantages of logging
Deforestation destroys the habitats of many species of plants and animals. The soil can erode more easily and nutrients can leach away leading to desertification. Carbon dioxide levels increase, so adding to the problems of global warming, and with the development of more residential areas and businesses comes pollution.

Page 54
Genetically modified food

FOR	AGAINST
insect-resistant crops	not safe for humans
larger crop yields	can harm the natural ecosystems
grow more easily in poor soils/climates	create gene flow into non-GM crops

Cars need to be banned from inner-city areas

FOR	AGAINST
more green areas	police cars / ambulances have limited access
less pollution	can adversely affect local economy
safer for shopping	high cost of developing public transport

Do you	Why?
1. find the weather much warmer?	Greenhouse Effect / too much CO_2 in the atmosphere
2. use recycled paper?	This helps to protect our forests.
3. shower instead of having a bath?	This helps to conserve our water.
4. walk short distances?	This helps reduce dependency on transport.
5. take a shopping bag to the supermarket?	This helps to conserve natural resources.
6. refuse to wear certain clothes or shoes?	Vegetarians, vegans and people who support animal rights often object to wearing leather or fur.
7. car pool?	Sharing cars helps to reduce your carbon footprint.
8. sort your rubbish into different bags?	This is part of recycling and conservation of our natural resources.

Page 56
1. G   2. E   3. D   4. A   5. G   6. B

Page 59
1. NO   2. NO   3. NOT GIVEN   4. YES   5. YES   6. YES   7. NOT GIVEN   8. NO

Page 60
1. x   2. ii   3. vii   4. iv   5. v   6. ix

Page 62
7. G - primitive   8. J - reference   9. D - mythical   10. I - tales

Page 63
It would be useful to develop the following suggestions:

Offer ideas explaining why people in Japan work past retirement age.

(This would be useful as background information and would be useful as part of your introduction.)

Explain why it is a good idea to retire early.

Give the advantages and advantages of retiring early.

State whether or not you agree with the Task 2 opinion.

Introduction
Nowadays, the trend is to move from the more rural areas to cities in the hope that this will create more opportunities for work. This essay discusses the advantages and disadvantages of moving to a city and then I will give my opinion on this.

Advantages
1. City life allows a person to be more in touch with the latest fashions and information.
2. City life can be more exciting with more opportunities presenting themselves than in the countryside.
3. Better opportunities for jobs and education can be found in a city.

Disadvantages
1. The pace of life in a city is much faster than in the countryside and more easily leads to a more stressful lifestyle and hence related health problems.
2. A real community atmosphere is much harder to find in the city and so it is much easier to feel lonely even when surrounded by people.
3. It is very easy to be led astray by the many temptations on offer in a city and lose track of who you really are.

Page 64
1 F   2A   3D   4E   5B   6G   7C

This paragraph is well written and the vocabulary is good. However, the ideas have not been developed. This one paragraph could be divided into 2 or 3 paragraphs.

Page 65

	Topic	Interested People / Groups
1.	endangered animals	zoologists, conservation organizations, park rangers, wildlife enthusiasts
2.	higher divorce rates	social workers, counselors, churches, governments, women's rights groups
3.	environmental problems	environmentalists, farmers, tourism operators
4.	sex education	health officials, doctors, teachers, schools, students, parents
5.	health issues	doctors, hospitals, health officials, parents, pharmaceutical companies

Page 66
In more recent times, people tend to travel by air if they need to travel further afield. However, this was not always the case because when people wanted to go on a long trip one hundred years ago, they would often have no choice but to go by ship. These trips would seem never-ending and were often quite exhausting.

Furthermore, second class passengers were less comfortable than first class passengers because they were not allowed to venture into the more exclusive areas. As a result, many preferred to travel by sea on vessels that had no class distinction.

Seventy years ago people still travelled by ship but since the 1960s international flights have become more popular. This is because they are safe, convenient and quick.

Page 67
1. B   2. A   3. B   4. B   5. B

1. relented   2. retracted   3. contracted   4. solve   5. distributing   6. cope   7. arranged

Page 68

For many years, educationalists have become increasingly concerned about the fierce competition to enter the best colleges and universities. As a result, it has become imperative to investigate the relative worth of both single-sex and coeducational schools to determine which style of education creates better opportunities. I am going to discuss this topic from both points of view and then conclude by giving my own opinion.

People in favour of single-sex schools argue that the environment offered in this type of schooling is far more conducive to learning. The main reason for this is that there are no distractions from the opposite sex and so students can feel more comfortable in their surroundings. It is also easier for students to select subjects of their choice without the influence of stereotypes seen in mixed schools where boys, more typically, study mathematics and girls study languages.

This is in direct contrast to people who are convinced that coeducational schools offer more opportunities for a better education. They believe that it is important for both sexes to study together because this provides a more realistic place to learn how to interact with the opposite sex. Most people after graduating from university will have to work side by side with members of both sexes and so important socialising skills can be learnt at school. Also, it has been suggested that the extra competition created in a mixed school between the two sexes seems to help girls be more competitive and study harder than they would in a single-sex school.

In conclusion, despite the obvious chances to socialise in mixed schools, I personally feel that single-sex schools can offer both a safer and more nurturing environment for students to learn and show their true scholastic potential.

Page 70

1. regulations   2. US$4,000,000   3. transferee   4. US$100,000   5. Lagos   6. representatives   7. tax
8. Central Bank / Bank of Nigeria   9. B   10. C

Page 72

1. No   2. No   3. Not Given   4. Yes   5. Not Given   6. No   7. Not Given   8. Marine Building
9. real estate developer   10. eliminate the causeway   11. "Polar Bear Swim"   12. dim sum   13. EcoWalk
14. paced   15 re-educated

Page 73

Sociologists have become increasingly concerned about rising levels of global stress and the negative effects this can have on divorce and suicide rates. As a result, it has been deemed necessary to develop ways to combat this social phenomenon. This essay looks at some of the causes of stress and will suggest some possible solutions.

While there are many reasons stress is increasing in society, several of the major causes are greater competition at work and financial worries. As educational standards rise around the world, it becomes more difficult to find a good job and a greater challenge to keep it. Indeed, as economies fall, and companies find themselves in a position of downsizing, the need to prove oneself has become an accepted necessity. Intimately connected with this is the need to earn enough money to support not only yourself but possibly a family as well. The rising cost of living combined with the lowering of bank rates creates more pressure to either get promotion in your existing job or find a better paid job.

There are several ways to help combat these causes but none of these ideas offer a quick fix. Instead, time and a lot of effort would be needed to begin to make inroads into these problems. First of all, it is essential for the government to raise the minimum wage so that at least some people would feel the benefits of these reforms. In addition, unemployment needs to be lowered and to do this the economy needs to be improved. To do this, the government needs to look carefully at the assets of the country and its workforce and develop the most effective methods of capitalising on its strengths.

All in all, it can be seen that this problem is not insurmountable but needs determination and patience from both the government and its people. By raising the minimum wage and lowering unemployment people will, over a period of time, begin to find that their lives are beginning to improve and find that life is not such a struggle. As stress slowly reduces people will become more confident within themselves and this will be reflected in their quality of work.

Page 75
1. A central issue   2. such as   3. However   4. As a result   5. subsequently   6. for instance
7. An additional benefit   8. Indeed

Formal education is seen by many people as the only way to become a well educated person. However, students are now realizing that education does not always have to come from the classroom. For instance, they can travel, work for a charity, or study non-academic skills during what is known as a gap year. This year offers them the chance to experience new things as well as time to reflect on their future career. A career that, perhaps, will change because of the time they spend experiencing the real world.

Page 77
NOTE – this is NOT a solution essay or an advantage / disadvantage essay. The Task 2 essay is agree / disagree and so the focus should be on whether or not you agree with the opinion - *A solution often put forward for reducing unemployment is for the government to enforce a lower retirement age.* The key point is how effective you think this solution is.

Many people support the idea of reducing the age of retirement because this is seen as a way to give younger people more opportunities to get a job. Furthermore, the fact that they are young would allow them to be trained more easily and accept innovation and new technology in a way that older people could not.

While these opinions seem convincing, they fail to take into consideration that older people have more experience not only within their area of expertise but also in society as a whole. Indeed, university graduates would find it very difficult to relate to the different kinds of relationships that exist in the business world.

Lastly, the attitude that older workers cannot change their vision or attitude because they are set in their ways is based on wishful thinking. We only need to look at some of our world leaders, both past and present, to see that age has no bearing on the ability to do well in their job.

Page 78
Many people would agree that cities are becoming more and more violent and guns are too easy to buy. News items regularly report robberies or murders where they were involved. As a consequence, people are now afraid to leave their homes at night or travel in taxis on their own. **I am going to discuss this topic** from both points of view and then conclude by giving my own opinion.

However, some people still feel that amendments to the existing legislations will have no effect on the increase in crime rate in cities. **They feel that** any increase in usage is the result of a poor economy rather than inadequate laws. Any improvement will, **therefore,** be the result of government intervention to rectify the economy rather than amendments to the existing laws.

In my opinion, however, I firmly believe that laws should be much tougher than they are now. **A good example of** a country that has shown that stricter laws do work is in the UK. The policemen walk the streets unarmed and gun related crime is much lower than in the USA where it seems anyone can buy them if they have the money. Other countries like Singapore have had similar results.

Another point of concern is that The number of homicides committed by children both at home and in school is increasing. Although the reasons for this social phenomenon are complex, the very least we can do is protect our children by introducing stronger laws. The people who own guns must be made more responsible for how and where they keep their firearms.

In conclusion, I firmly believe that the best way to make the streets safer is by introducing new government legislation to make it more difficult to buy weapons. Let us follow the example of countries where such measures have already been adopted and the results clearly seen.

N.B. Notice that in this example the text has been changed slightly to reduce the number of times the word "gun" has been used. However, the context is still very clear. Compare this with the original text to see how this has been done. Now try to think of ways to reduce the number of times the word "law" has been used.

Page 79
If you are looking for a unique city to visit in Southeast Asia, Ho Chi Minh City in Vietnam would be a fascinating destination. Located on the Mekong River, it was once an important trading center for the French. Although

they eventually left the country, their influence and culture can still be felt. For instance, many of the buildings in the city are built in the French style and many people, especially the older generations, can still speak the language very well. After an enjoyable day visiting the museums and monuments documenting the country's long – and often bloody – history, treat yourself to some French cuisine in one of the numerous expensive hotels and restaurants to be found in the city. If you are on a smaller budget, some of the cafes still serve colonial-style bread and pastries.

Page 84
1. 6bn acres   2. 2.8bn acres   3. 1.5 bn acres   4. 0 bn acres   5. A   6. B   7. B   8. D

Page 86
1. Yes   2. Yes   3. Yes   4. No   5. Yes   6. Not Given   7. Yes

Word Focus
1. C   2. E   3. F   4. B   5. A   6. D

Page 88
1. explosives and gasoline   2. Belgium   3. 50,000   4. 18 metres   5. (Approximately) 2,000
6. collisions   7. channel   8. Thousands   9. one-fifth   10. trapped

Page 89
1. I feel, however, that   2. The argument against studying in a foreign country mainly focuses on the fact
3. Indeed,   4. In addition   5. While it is true that a certain degree of sacrifice is needed,   6. In addition,
7. In fact,   8. To conclude,

Page 90
Global Warming
1. E   2. C

Childhood Obesity
1. C   2. E

Bullying in Schools
1. E   2. C

Page 91
1. Increase in industrialisation
2. Increase in the production of electricity
3. Better infrastructure
4. A rise in transportation
5. Demand for more land because of the need to grow biofuels and build residential homes
6. Deforestation
7. The increase in CO_2 in the atmosphere
8. The dramatic increase in global warning can be attributed to one main factor

Page 92
For many years, animal conservationists have felt that not enough is being done to protect endangered animals from the increasing dangers of poaching and habitat destruction. However, continued investment in zoos has raised certain ethical questions and has led to discussions about the benefits and drawbacks of these establishments. In this essay, I will discuss both sides of this topic and then give my opinion.

One of the key advantages of zoos is that they encourage conservation of endangered and protected species through captive breeding programmes. Without this help, many species would now be extinct but instead they survive within the protective walls of various zoos around the world. In this way, it might be possible to reintroduce these animals into the wild in the future. Zoos also offer a wonderful opportunity to educate people about different animals that they might, perhaps, never see in the wild. This will, hopefully, make people realise the value of protecting these animals from the terrible destruction of their habitats that is happening at the moment.

However, despite strict regulations on how animals should be kept, many zoos, especially those in developing countries, keep their animals in cramped cages and treat them in a less than perfect way. This can result partly from a lack of knowledge on how to take care of the animals but also from the high costs involved in feeding them and providing a suitable environment for them to live in. Many of the animals also lose their natural instincts and would never survive in the wild if released there.

All in all, I believe that we should continue to support the development and maintenance of zoos as they help counterbalance the rapid destruction of large areas of land that were once home to many forms of wildlife.

Page 93
A
This sentence is illogical and so the order of information needs to change. Remember that the focus is on the graduates **not** the university. It is the graduates that are more 'efficient and effective' **not** the university. If rewritten we could write:

To conclude, I believe that graduates who have been given the **proper** knowledge and skills by their university are more effective and efficient whatever tasks **are** given to them in the workplace.

However, you may also have noted the following errors in the original sentence:

1. 'properly (proper) - grammar error
2. 'tasks given' (tasks are given) - grammar error

B
In conclusion, universities should focus on **providing students in-depth knowledge** accompanied by appropriate skills in line with the **carer** they decide to take. Although providing more information would be practical **yet** expertise in a particular field would tend to matter more.

The various problems are:

1. 'providing students in-depth knowledge' (providing students with an in-depth knowledge of their subject) - grammar error
2. 'carer' (career) - spelling mistake
3. 'yet' (this is not needed in the sentence) - grammar error

C
In conclusion, universities need to make changes to the subjects and courses on offer to allow **student** to learn directly the knowledge and skills **need** for a better **career life**. Hopefully, this move will **increase** the percentage of jobless citizens in the world today.

The various problems are:

1. 'student' (students) - grammar error
2. 'need' (needed) - grammar error
3. 'career life' (career) - poor vocabulary selection
4. 'increase' (decrease) - poor logic

D
To conclude, from my personal **points** of view, universities should impart **its** knowledge and practical skills, that are relevant in the workplace because, with more **knowledge and skills students will adjust quickly in his** new job.

The various problems are:

1. 'points' (point) - grammar error
2. 'its' (their) - grammar error
3. 'knowledge and skills' (not needed) - repeated vocabulary
4. 'students will adjust quickly in his' (students will adjust quickly in their) - grammar error

Page 94
1. Many scholars are now convinced   2. therefore,   3. With this in mind,   4. My first recommendation would be to provide   5. for example,   6. Another way to help address this problem would be if   7. In addition   8. Finally,   9. All in all, I am firmly convinced

Page 95
The best conclusion is example **B**

Introduction
It is often felt that travel is the best form of education and so many people travel abroad whenever money and time allows. However, this attitude suggests that their own country is seen as a second-class country with nothing to offer them. This is clearly not the case and so ways must be found to change this attitude and encourage people to travel more in their own countries. In the following essay, I will offer a number of ways to help address this situation.

Conclusion
To conclude, in the examples presented here it can be clearly seen that the government has to treat this social phenomenon as a serious issue and put more effort into encouraging domestic tourism. The establishment of both local and national tourist offices designed to offer tour information will be one step towards solving this problem. A key factor in solving this problem is also price; if tour operators could offer affordable tours, people would think twice before travelling overseas.

Page 96

		YES	NO
1.	Include the conclusion as the last part of the main body		X
2.	Use the conclusion to create a feeling of wanting to know more		X
3.	Restate the topic direction	X	
4.	Put extra information or evidence to support your ideas into the conclusion		X
5.	The conclusion should summarize the main body	X	
6.	Start the conclusion by writing, "In conclusion"	X	
7.	Put the conclusion in the last paragraph	X	

"In conclusion" is acceptable but rather boring.
Conclusion 2 is much better. Conclusion 1 has multiple problems: it repeats large sections of text from the body, and it gives an example (and to make matters worse, it's a new example, and much too personalised).

TASK 2 Questions

CULTURE
1. When visiting foreign countries, visitors should take full advantage of learning the culture and traditions of that country.
2. Why are some people not interested in learning about the culture and traditions of a country?
3. What are some ways to learn about the culture and traditions of a country?

EDUCATION
1. In some countries, students who do not behave are asked to leave the school permanently. In other countries, they can return to their school after a suspension period. Discuss both options and give your opinion.
2. Some people think that the education system should prepare students for employment, while others believe it has other functions.
   Discuss both sides and then give your own opinion.
3. Some people claim that students should focus on the subjects that they are interested in, or best at, while others believe that students should learn all school subjects.
   Discuss both sides of this argument and give your own opinion.
4. Some people argue that teachers should make the choice about the subjects and lesson contents for their classes. Others think this should be decided by the government.
   To what extent do you agree or disagree?
5. Some people think that young people should go to university, while other people say that they should skip university and go straight to work.
   To what extent do you agree?
6. Many people these days believe that young people should travel abroad for a year after finishing high school. But others think it is a waste of time and money.
   What is your opinion?
7. In some countries, some school leavers choose to work or travel for a year between finishing secondary school and attending university.
   Discuss the advantages and disadvantages of this and then give your opinion.

EMPLOYMENT
1. Some people think that elderly people should be forced to retire at a certain age, such as 65. Others say that people should be allowed to work for as long as they are able and want to.
   Discuss both sides of this argument and then give your own opinion.
2. Nowadays, people in some countries can choose to live and work anywhere they want, because of the improvement in communication technology and transport.
   Discuss the advantages and disadvantages of this and then give your own opinion.

ENTERTAINMENT
1. Some museums and art galleries charge admission fees, while others have free entry.
   Do you think the advantages of free admission outweigh the disadvantages?

ENVIRONMENT - problems
1. Some people believe that environmental problems are too big for individuals to deal with, and that action is needed from the government while others think that individuals should take some action.
   Discuss both sides of the argument and then give your opinion.

ENVIRONMENT – traffic
1. In countries all over the world, the volume of road traffic is increasing at a faster rate than new roads can be built. What are the causes of this problem?
   What are some potential solutions?

NATURAL RESOURCES - energy

1. Oil and coal are the main sources of energy in many countries. However, in some countries the use of renewable sources of energy, such as solar or wind energy, are encouraged.
   Is it a positive or a negative development?

RETIREMENT

1. In some countries the elderly are put into nursing homes rather than being taken care of by their family.
   Do you see this as a positive or a negative development?

SOCIETY - consumerism

1. Nowadays, people live in a society where consumer goods are relatively cheaper to buy.
   Do you think the advantages far outweigh the disadvantages?
2. People in the past would always repair damaged products. However, nowadays, people like to throw them out and purchase new products.
   What are the reasons for this?
   What problems might this cause?

SOCIETY - entertainment

1. Some people believe that sports people and entertainers are paid too much money and that professional workers such as doctors, nurses and teachers who make greater contribution to the society should be paid more.
   What is your opinion?

SOCIETY - government

1. Some people believe that it is the government's responsibility to take care of every citizen who is disadvantaged.
   What is your opinion?

SOCIETY - music

1. Some people think music plays an important role in society. Others think it is simply a form of entertainment.
   Discuss both sides of this argument and give your own opinion.

SOCIETY - obesity

1. Obesity is an increasing problem in today's society. Some people say that the government should put a higher tax on fast foods in order to solve this problem.
   Discuss the advantages and disadvantages of this and then give your own opinion.

SOCIETY - stress

1. Some people believe that the fast pace and stress of modern life is having a negative effect on families.
   To what extent do you agree or disagree?

SOCIETY - urban sprawl

1. As cities get bigger, many people do not know their neighbours and the sense of community is being lost.
   What problems does this cause?
   What are some potential solutions?

TECHNOLOGY

1. The range of technology available for some individuals, and countries, will increase the gap between the rich and poor. Others think it is having an opposite effect.
   What is your opinion?

DATE DUE	RETURNED
JUN 0 8 2015	JUN 1 9 2015
JUL 2 2 2015	JUL 2 1 2015
SEP 2 9 2015	
OCT 1 3 2015	
OCT 1 4 2015	OCT 1 3 2015
JAN 2 6 2016	JAN 2 5 2016
JUL 2 1 2016	AUG 0 3 2016
	FEB 1 5 2017
MAR 1 2017	
JUL 2 0 2017	JUL 2 1 2017

CPSIA information can be obtained at www.ICGtesting.com
Printed in the USA
LVOW02s0109161214

419023LV00009B/149/P